John Habberton

The Scripture Club of Valley Rest

Sketches of Everybody's Neighbors

John Habberton

The Scripture Club of Valley Rest
Sketches of Everybody's Neighbors

ISBN/EAN: 9783337418083

Printed in Europe, USA, Canada, Australia, Japan

Cover: Foto ©Thomas Meinert / pixelio.de

More available books at **www.hansebooks.com**

THE

SCRIPTURE CLUB

OF VALLEY REST

OR

SKETCHES OF EVERYBODY'S NEIGHBOURS

By THE AUTHOR OF
"*The Barton Experiment,*" "*Helen's Babies,*" Etc.

NEW YORK

G. P. PUTNAM'S SONS

182 FIFTH AVENUE.

—

1877

CONTENTS.

3

CHAPTER VIII.

CHAPTER IX.

CHAPTER X.

CHAPTER XI.

SCRIPTURE CLUB.

CHAPTER I.

A LIBERAL MOVEMENT.

THE success of the Second Church of Valley Rest was too evident to admit of doubt, and there seemed to be no one who begrudged the infant society its prosperity. Most of its members had come to the village from that Western city known to all its inhabitants as being the livest on the planet, and they had brought their business wits with them. At first they worshiped with the members of the First Church, established forty years before, and with an Indian or two still among its members; but it soon became evident to old members and new that no single society could be of sufficient

theological elasticity to contain all the worship-
ers who assembled in the old building. There
were differences of opinion, which, though
courteously expressed, seemed great enough to
claim conscientious convictions for their bases ;
so with a Godspeed as hearty as their welcome
had been, the newer attendants organized a
new society. They were strong, both numerically and financially, so within a year they had
erected and paid for a costly and not hideous
church building, settled a satisfactory pastor, and
organized a Sunday-school, three prayer-meet-
ings, and a sewing society. The activity of the
new church became infectious, and stimulated
the whole community to good works ; occasionally one of the other societies would endeavor to
return some of the spiritual favors conferred by
the Second Church, but so leisurely were the
movements of the older organizations that before they could embody a suggestion in an experience the new church would have discerned it
afar off and put it into practical operation.

It was in the rapid manner alluded to that the Second Church came finally by a feature which long and gloriously distinguished it. It was 11.50 by the church clock one Sunday morning when Mrs. Buffle, wife of the great steamboat owner, who made his home at Valley Rest, noticed her husband's face suddenly illumine as if he had just imagined a model for the best lake packet that ever existed; it was only 12.10, by the same time-piece, when about thirty of the solid members of the church, remaining after service, gathered in a corner of the otherwise vacant building, and agreed to Mr. Buffle's proposal that there should be organized a Bible class especially for adults.

"When you think of it," explained the projector, "it really seems as if there'd be no end to its usefulness. I call myself as orthodox a man as you can find in any church, anywhere, but there's lots of things in the Bible that I'm not posted on. I suppose it's the same with all of you ; each of you may have thought a great deal on some single subject, but you're not up in everything—you haven't sat under preachers who talk about everything."

"There aren't many preachers who *dare* to preach about everything," remarked young lawyer Scott, who had in marked degree the youthful appetite for the strongest mental food, and the youthful assumption that whatever can be swallowed is bound to be digested.

"Nor that dares to say what he really believes," added Captain Maile, who had that peculiar mind, not unknown in theology and in politics, which loves a doubt far more dearly than it does a demonstration.

"Preachers are like the rest of us," said Mr. Buffle; "they haven't time to study everything, and they have to take a good deal on the say-so of somebody else; a good many things they may be mistaken about, but they'd better have *some* idea on a subject than none at all; once get a notion into their heads and it'll roll around and make them pay attention to it once in a while. And that's just what *we* need, I think, and it's what brought this Bible class idea into my mind. Each of us will express our minds on whatever may be the subject of the day's lesson, and we'll learn how many ways there are of looking at it. No one of us may change his mind all at once, but if he gets out of his own rut for an hour in a week, he'll find it a little wider and no less safer when he drops into it again."

"And perhaps he may get it so wide that there'll be room enough in it for three or four, or half-a-dozen Christians to walk in it side by side, without kicking each other, or eyeing each other suspiciously," suggested Brother Radley, whose golden text always was, "It is good for brethren to dwell together in unity."

"*That's* it!" exclaimed Mr. Buffle, his eyes brightening suddenly. "That's it! But I don't intend to do all the talking, gentlemen. I suggest that such of us as like the idea sign our names to an agreement to meet every Sunday

for the purpose specified, and that we immediately afterward proceed to elect a teacher."

"I don't wish to dampen any honest enthu-
siasm for Biblical research;" said Dr. Humbletop, a genial ex-minister; "but from some remarks which have been made it would seem as
if doubt—perhaps honest, but doubt for all that
—were to have more to do than faith with the
motive of the proposed association. What we
need—what *I* feel to need, at least, and what I
believe is the case with all who are here present
—is to be rooted and grounded in the faith
which we profess. I would move, therefore,
that if the class is to be informally organized in
the manner proposed by Brother Buffle, that at
least the creed of our church be appended to
the document to which signatures are to be
affixed."

"Mr. Chairman," exclaimed Mr. Alleman
(Principal of the Valley Rest Academy, and
suspected of certain fashionable heresies), "I
object. In our congregation—here in this small

gathering, in fact—is a large sprinkling of gentlemen who are not members of the church, and
who do not accept our creed, though they enjoy worshiping with us : Brother Humbletop's
resolution, if put into effect, would exclude from
the proposed teachings the very class of men
that we profess to believe are most in need of
religious instruction. The churches are so
rigid that a thinking man can scarcely gain admission to them without lying, actually or con-
structively : don't let us, in a class like that
proposed, follow the example of the Pharisees,
those very flowers of orthodoxy—and 'lay on
men's shoulders burdens grievous to be borne.'
If our religion is what we claim it is, let us
open our gates wide enough to admit every one
who is at all interested to study God's ways as
made known through the scriptures."

" Don't trouble yourself," said Captain Maile,
who was as dyspeptic in body as in mind, but
was also a keen observer of human nature ; " I
don't see but saints need converting as badly as

sinners do, and there's enough of *them* to keep you busy. We sinners can find a gathering place somewhere else—perhaps the sexton will think the furnace-room the proper place for us —and we'll take Christian hospitality and greatheartedness as our first subject for discussion."

" You won't do anything of the kind," exclaimed Squire Woodhouse, one of the old settlers who had joined himself to the Second Church to avoid being tormented about what some of the members of the First Church termed his rationalism. " You're going to meet with us, blow us up all you like, teach us anything you can, and make us better in any way you know how to. God Almighty's kingdom isn't any four-acre lot with a high stone wall and a whole string of warnings to trespassers ; his kingdom takes in all out-doors ; every man alive is his child, and got a right to come and go in his Father's house, even if he don't sit on the same style of chair or creep under the same kind of bedclothes that his brothers do. If he

don't like the meat, or bread, or dessert that
somebody else is eating, the table's so full of
other good things that he *can't* go hungry unless he insists upon it. There isn't one of you
but's got more religion and brains than any of
the twelve apostles ever had; but none of *them*
were ever turned out of *the* Bible class, though
one of them, who was a thief, was man enough
to stay away of his own accord, and voluntarily
go to judgment."

"Churches wouldn't be near so full if all
thieves followed Judas's example," was the un-
gracious remark with which Captain Maile received this handsome speech; a hearty laugh
took the sting out of the captain's insinuation,
however. Meanwhile Mr. Buffle had torn a
leaf out of a hymn-book, scrawled a form of
agreement thereupon, and passed it around for
signatures. When the paper reached Dr.
Humbletop, that gentleman said:

" Brethren, I sign this paper in the hope that
we shall work together for the honor and glory

of God; but I distinctly avow and reserve the right to withdraw at any time, should such time come, when my conscience forbids me any longer to attend."

Several others, among them Insurance President Lottson and Mr. Stott, the well-to-do builder, announced the same reservation, but no one entirely declined to sign. Then Mr. Buffle moved the election of a teacher, and the choice fell upon Deacon Bates, a man of unabused conscience, pure life, extreme orthodoxy, and an aimless curiosity (which he mistook for thought) about things Biblical and spiritual. Then Mr. Buffle arose and said:

" Mr. Chairman—Mr. Teacher, I mean—time is money in the church as well as in the world. It's only 12.30; Sunday-school won't be out until 1.30. I move we select a lesson, and go right to work."

The motion was put and carried, and in a second Dr. Humbletop was upon his feet.

" I propose," said he, " that after the offering

of a prayer—an essential which seems to have been overlooked by our brethren so zealous in good works—that we proceed to the consideration of the Epistle of Paul to the Romans. Let us sit at the feet of one, the latchet of whose shoes no other theologian was ever worthy to unloose, and let us there seek those truths which shall make us wise unto salvation. Let us make ourselves fully acquainted with God's plan for the redemption of sinful man."

" I move as a substitute," said Mr. Alleman, " that we begin with the Sermon on the Mount, and learn from the Master instead of the servant."

The place was a church and the occasion was the study of the Scriptures. But the attendants were only human and they recognized the conditions necessary to a fight with many indications of satisfaction; faces lightened up, eyes rapidly increased in luster, and lips unconsciously parted in the manner natural to persons who are gradually abandoning themselves to the influence of an impending pleasure. Men sitting to the right, left, and front of the apparent contestants twisted their necks until their eyes commanded the scene ; while good old Major Brayme, who was rather deaf, and had got into a corner for his neuralgia's sake, scented the battle afar off and limped around to a front seat.

" The question is on the amendment," said the leader, "unless some brother has still another amendment to offer."

Nobody spoke ; as Captain Maile afterward explained, " 'twasn't anybody else's fight." Besides, Valley Rest was peopled by the race peculiar to all other portions of this terrestrial ball, and one of the instincts of that race, whether savage or civilized, is that it is far more pleasing to be a spectator than a participant in an altercation.

" Mr. Leader," said Mr. Alleman after a moment of silence, "in support of my amendment I wish to say that no one more enthusiastically

admires than I do the remarkable, almost
unique, logical ability of the apostle; but the
very reason which prompted him to give forth
that wonderful letter to the Romans is the one
which I offer in opposition to our studying that
same epistle. Paul was originally a shrewd
man of the world, and his conversion did not
deprive him of his common sense and tact.
Writing to the church at Rome—a church
whose members, judging by the Roman mental
constitution, must have been gained through
appeals logical rather than emotional—he met
them upon their own ground, and taught them
and grounded them in belief through those faculties in them which were most easily reached,
and which, more than any others, would retain
the impressions formed upon them. Of all that
Paul taught we profess to be convinced; of what
Christ taught we are not so well informed, for
the reason that it is Paul, rather than Christ,
who is preached from the pulpit. But here we
are in a world and a state of society in which,

for righteousness' sake, we are less helped by logically drawn dogma than by earnest injunction and pure example. We *do* believe; what we need is to learn to lead the new life which that belief implies; we need to have asserted, explained, and impressed upon us the simple but comprehensive rules and gracious promises which Jesus enounced during his life. The Sermon on the Mount begins with the Beatitudes; which of us really *believes* in them as we do in Paul's argument to the Romans? It continues and concludes with a number of moral injunctions, all of which we practically reject, or at least neglect; yet these bear directly on our daily intercourse with our fellow-men, and our daily acts of all sorts. Why, St. Paul himself apparently preached after this same model when he had to talk to men of the world whose intelligence was not confined to a single groove, for we read that when he preached—talked—to Felix, the governor, he reasoned of righteousness, temperance, and the judgment to come.

Therefore I move, for the good of those here assembled, and for the glory of God, that this class proceed to the study of the Sermon on the Mount."

There was a perceptible rustle and an active interchange of winks and head-shakings as Mr. Alleman closed; but a dead silence was restored as Dr. Humbletop slowly rose to his feet, cleared his throat, adjusted his newly-polished glasses, and raised his voice.

" My dear friends," said he, " having been an humble but earnest follower of the Lord Jesus Christ for nearly half a century, I need not on this occasion enter into a defense of myself against any possible insinuation of lack of faith. Nor will any one doubt that I apprehend the great value of the Sermon on the Mount; some of you will, perhaps, recall a series of sermons which I preached a few years ago upon the Beatitudes. But Jesus Christ was not merely a moral teacher; his great work was to redeem the world from death by offering himself as a propitiation for their sins, and submitting himself unto death, even the shameful death of the cross.   His teachings were great, he spake as man never spake before, but all this is as naught compared with the great work which he finished upon Calvary.   It is *this* that we need to study; it is for this we should love and adore him.   'God so loved the world, that he gave his only-begotten Son, that whosoever believeth in him should not perish, but have eternal life.'"

"I should like to ask Brother Humbletop if personal salvation is the highest motive with which we should study the Bible?" said Mr. Alleman.

It was evident that the question was a poser to the good doctor; the very convexity and luster of his glasses served only to make his eyes stare more aimlessly at nothing for a moment or two.   He recovered himself, however, and replied :

"God, in his generosity, and doubtless in

view of the needs of sinful humanity, has ordered that the salvation of mankind should have been the principal object of Christ's coming upon earth; I am not here to criticise my Maker."

"And you know that no one else is," remarked Mr. Alleman, with not inexcusable acerbity.

"Question!" exclaimed several voices. The leader put the question, and the amendment of Mr. Alleman was adopted by a considerable majority. Again Dr. Humbletop got upon his feet.

"My dear friends," said he, "I regret at this early hour to part from an association from which I had fondly hoped to derive spiritual benefit, but my sense of duty impels me to take such a step; the vote of the class seems to indicate an estimate of Christ to which I should never dare to commit myself—an estimate against which I must always protest. Personally, I hold you all in high esteem; you shall al-

2

ways be remembered by me at the throne of grace, but upon the prime essential of Christian fraternity we seem hopelessly at variance. In one way I doubt not that your deliberations will tend toward good, but that way is not the best way, and I must therefore regret it. I shall consider it my duty to take steps toward the organization of a class upon what I conceive to be a Christian basis, and in that class I shall always be ready to heartily welcome any of you. Salvation through the atonement of Christ is the central truth of the Bible; a body of students who examine the Word from any other standpoint may be perfectly sincere and in earnest, and they may constitute what may without unkind meaning be called a Scripture Club, but they can never claim to be regarded as a Bible class, in the proper acceptation of the term."

The doctor gathered his cloak, hat, and cane, and retired with a graceful but dignified bow; the class rose to its feet in some confusion, and Squire Woodhouse exclaimed:

" Scripture Club, eh? Well, it's a good name."

" That's so," said Mr. Alleman ; " let's adopt it, and show the blessed old man that names can't change natures."

A general assent was sounded; not so noisy a one, perhaps, as that with which the Dutch patriots of three hundred years ago accepted the designation of " Beggars," cast at them by Spain, and destined to recoil upon those who bestowed it; but the acclamation was nevertheless more earnest and demonstrative than is common in churches, and it was perhaps well that in the midst of it the dismissal of the Sunday-school compelled parents who were members of the " Club " to hurry out in search of their children.

CHAPTER II.

SOME SPIRITUAL DIFFERENCES.

THE next meeting of the Scripture Club of Valley Rest was impatiently looked forward to by all the club members. Although there were at that time plenty of political theories to quarrel over, two or three fine projects for new lines of lake navigation, and at least a dozen for making of the neighboring city the greatest Western rival to New York, conversation on these subjects was only fitful on the boats which carried the business men of Valley Rest between their homes and the city. Before the second Sunday of the existence of the class, each member had in mind at least one religious topic upon which he wanted full, exhaustive, and decisive discussion; he also in his innermost heart, and sometimes on his lips, had the

settled conviction that he was just the man
to speak the decisive word, and thus readjust
human thought to the newly-discovered requirements of eternal truth.

Nor was excitement on religious topics confined to the members of the club. Not a day
of the week passed without bringing to Deacon
Bates a new candidate for admission. First
came Mr. Hopper, who took enthusiastic delight
in whatever was new, whether in religion, politics, medical theories, or popular smoking to-
baccos. As Mr. Hopper was a rich man, good
Deacon Bates hastily assured him that the class
would be delighted to have him as a member,
and Mr. Hopper graciously responded by offering to read at the very first meeting a seven-
teen-page paper, from a very heavy but comparatively new quarterly, on "The True Location of the Holy Sepulchre." Then came Mr.
Jodderel, who had once defrayed the entire cost
of producing a bulky pamphlet, the motive of
which was the probable final settlement of all

departed spirits, in renewed bodies, on some
one of the terrestrial globes which he believed
had been in preparation from the foundation of
the world. Mr. Jodderel more than hinted that
he would like to see considerable attention
given to this topic in the new class, and though
good Leader Bates trembled at the thought,
having heard the same subject discussed in season and out of season ever since Mr. Jodderel
had made the coming peerless city of the West
his place of business, he was true to the sentiment which had led to the formation of the
class, and therefore gave Mr. Jodderel a hearty
fraternal welcome. Then, like Nicodemus,
there came by night, and from fear of the orthodox, Brother Prymm, to whom the slightest
letter of the law was of more importance than
the whole of the spirit thereof. He had made
the matter of joining the class a subject of
special prayer, he said, and had made up his
mind that if it were really the intention of the
members to encourage free speech and honest-

ly search for the actual truth regarding the will
of God, it was his duty to join the class, and
serve his blessed Master to the extent of his
poor abilities. Mr. Maddle came next, and
Leader Bates' heart gladdened to receive him,
for Mr. Maddle was one of the most successful
organizers in the State ; he had planned and
executed at least two remarkably successful
campaigns in the local political field, and had
reorganized, out of nothing, more than one
shapeless business enterprise so admirably that
the backers thereof could not learn what they
had expended, nor could the creditors discern
what they themselves had received. With such
a man behind him, Leader Bates rose superior
to his own fears of the possible disintegration
which the diversity of views of his fellow-mem-
bers had seemed to make possible. And then,
as if providentially sent to give the class the
impress and protection of the highest order of
mentality, came Dr. Fahrenglohz, Ph.D., Göt-
tingen, who had additional repute as being a

good physician and a man who always paid his
bills.   All these were present at the opening
hour of the next meeting, and with them came
several people of the class which yields capital
listeners, and proves the wondrous capacity of
the human mind for absorbing information without ever being moved to lend any of it again
to others.

The meeting was opened with prayer.   Deacon Bates remarked prefatorily that such would
be the proper thing in a class composed of
adults, and then he looked around hesitatingly
for the proper man to make the first formal
committal of the class into the hands of the
Lord ; but Squire Woodhouse saved him the
trouble by springing to his feet and volunteer-
ing to Heaven an address so concise that there
remained nothing unsaid.   Then Bibles were
distributed, and opened at the fifth chapter of
Matthew's Gospel, and every one looked un-
speakably profound, though Mr. Hopper had
the presence of mind to place his hand beneath

his coat-tails and take hold of the review containing the paper on " The True Location of the Holy Sepulchre," so as to be ready in case occasion offered.

" Let us begin with the beatitudes," said the leader. " 'Blessed are the poor in spirit, for theirs is the kingdom of heaven.' By the way, I would suggest that each member speaks in the order of his sitting. Mr. Lottson," continued Deacon Bates, addressing the insurance president, "whom do you suppose Jesus referred to as ' the poor in spirit ' ? "

" Before answering that question," said Mr. Lottson, " I think attention should be called to a passage in the opening of the chapter. It is said that ' When he was set, *his disciples* came unto him. And he opened his mouth and taught *them*, saying,' etc. Now, before we try to understand this beautiful succession of blessings, we should realize whom they were spoken to—to the disciples, who had left all and followed him, and therefore to a set of men to

whom he could say things which it would be
nonsensical for him to say to the common
people and business men around him. The
disciples were out of business, and lived on
their friends—it was right enough for them to do
so under the circumstances, but for this very
reason Jesus told them the things which nobody
else could understand. This sermon was
preached to self-forgetting preachers, not to
men who had to make their living and take the
world as they found it; and I suppose the
first beatitude meant to them just what it said.
They were poor in spirit—any man has to be,
if he be willing to go around without a cent in
his pocket—but to pay them for it he gave them
the kingdom of heaven, that is, the church of
which Christ is prophet, priest, and king. It's
the greatest charge in the world; all business
enterprises are nothing in comparison with it;
but Jesus showed his divine nature by giving
them this, for while they managed it splendidly,
it's the only great affair in the world that a lot

of poor-spirited men could manage without running it into the ground."

"That depends upon what 'poor in spirit' means," remarked Squire Woodhouse. "President Lottson seems to think it's the same thing as mean-spirited, but if it is, I can tell him that there's more money for that kind of chaps in other businesses. Now I'm a farmer—my principal crop is hay, and when my barn burned down last winter with eleven tons loose and forty odd tons pressed, and I went to the insur——"

"The members will please speak as called upon," said the leader, whose watchful ear imagined it detected a personality in the immediate future of the Squire's address. Squire Woodhouse subsided after a soft whisper to his right-hand neighbor, which caused that gentleman to notice that President Lottson's face was flushing a little, and his lips touching each other more firmly than usual.

"It seems to me," said Mr. Radley, who was next called upon, "that the passage means just what it says. The kingdom of heaven means the place we all hope to get to some day, and the poor in spirit are the people who aren't touchy and don't put on airs. Christ was a man of this kind himself, and he knew by experience what he was talking about."

"Then how did he come to call a lot of good church members vipers?" demanded Squire Woodhouse, before the leader could bring him to order.

"Because they *were* vipers," answered Mr. Radley. "Being poor in spirit — humble — doesn't need to keep anybody from telling the truth. It's your *high*-spirited chaps that do most of the lying in the world—they do in business circles anyway."

"Next," said Deacon Bates, and Captain Maile lifted up his voice.

"Judging by the notions most people have of the kingdom of heaven," said he, "I don't think anybody but poor-spirited people can ever want to go there."

Next in order came Mr. Jodderel, and, as he afterward told his wife, he breathed a small thank-offering to Heaven for preparing so perfect an occasion for the presentation of his own theological pet.

" I don't wonder," he said, " that my military friend turns up his nose at the home-made heaven of most people, but I want him to understand that it was no such place that the Lord was talking about. What did he mean when he said, ' Come, ye blessed of my Father, and inherit the kingdom prepared for you from the foundation of the world ' ? What sensible man imagines that the kingdom he spoke of meant any such place as Christians talk about, or even the place where the Lord himself is ? It can't be the latter, for *that* wasn't prepared from the foundation of the world ; it existed long before, and didn't need any preparation. If he prepared the kingdom from the foundation of the world, and made the sun, moon, and stars when he founded the world—

a fact which I fully and implicitly believe because it is recorded in the inspired Word—the
kingdom must be in some other sphere. And
if, as astronomers say, and I have no reason to
doubt, these spheres are worlds, a great deal
like ours, we will have material bodies when we
go to them."

"And poor spirits?" queried the insurance
president.

"Yes!" exclaimed Mr. Jodderel fearlessly.
"We can't go there without first dying here,
and I never yet saw a man on his death-bed
who thought a high spirit, or what men call a
high spirit, had ever done him any good."

President Lottson tried to swallow a sigh
which was a little too quick for him ; he had
once or twice imagined himself on his own
death-bed, and had gained thereon some practical intimations which he had made haste to
forget when he got back to business. Mr.
Prymm, who sat next to Mr. Jodderel, cleared
his throat and said :

"I think we owe Mr. Lottson our thanks for calling our attention to an important fact which has escaped general notice. The sermon *was* undoubtedly preached to the disciples, and should be considered accordingly; a great many mistakes of interpretation are doubtless due to the habit of Christians in taking to themselves every saying of the Lord and his prophets. I confess that the view advanced is so new a one to me that I am unable at present to express any opinion upon it, but I derive already this benefit from it—I learn anew how necessary it is to pay close attention to the letter of the Word."

"Then," said young Mr. Waggett, who sat next Mr. Prymm, and who was principally remarkable for undeviating devotion to Number One, "then the passage has nothing to do with the great affair of the salvation of our own souls."

"Supposing it hasn't," said Squire Woodhouse, in spite of the warning glance of the leader, " Sunday isn't a business day, and if we want to talk about some of our best friends then there's no harm in doing so, nor any time wasted either."

" Brother Scott," said Deacon Bates. The young lawyer, who had been exerting over himself a degree of control that was simply terrible, considering his temptations to interruption, said :

" May it please the class : There are some evident misunderstandings abroad. Mr. Lottson's position is untenable, as the context of the same sermon proves ; no examination, according to the rules of evidence, can fail to prove that the sermon was addressed to the whole people. The passage cannot mean literally what it says, as Mr. Radley thinks, because literally it is illogical, and had such been its intention it could never have been accepted by that consistent apologist for the integrity of the Scriptures, the Apostle Paul, whose mind was so marvelously under control of the legal instinct. Captain Maile's assumption as to the general idea of heaven is utterly without support from fact ; for poverty of spirit is not the prevailing characteristic of those whose opinions of heaven are verbally made manifest. As for Mr. Jodderel's proposition, it involves the literal accuracy of the Book of Genesis, which many orthodox Christians are unprepared to admit. Mr. Prymm's notion that the sayings of Jesus may be wrongly taken by individuals, as applying to themselves, is not in accordance with logical deductions from other portions of Holy Writ. And how can Mr. Waggett sustain his position that there is *any* eternal truth that is not necessary to salvation? "

A soft chorus of long-drawn breaths followed the delivery of this speech, and then Squire Woodhouse said :

" Well, now that you've knocked all the rest down, what are you going to do yourself? "

" That," replied Lawyer Scott, evidently pleased by the compliment but puzzled by the

3

question, " cannot be answered as easily as it
is asked, and I must beg the gentleman's indulgence until I have time to prepare my
case."

Mr. Buffle, founder of the class, was next in
order, and admitted that he could not see that
Jesus, being a clear-headed man, could ever
have meant anything but what he said. He,
Mr. Buffle, always said what he meant, no matter whether he was talking to preachers, ship-
pers, or the deck-hands on his own boats ; he
had found that if a man said exactly what he
meant, the stupidest of people could understand
him, while smarter people needed no more.
He would consider himself a fool if he talked
over the head of any one who was listening to
him, and of course Jesus couldn't have been
foolish. He was very glad, though, to listen
to the many different views that had been advanced on the subject ; they proved just what
he had always believed, that men would learn
more about a thing by hearing all sides of it

than he could from the smartest talker alive who
knew only one side. He liked the liberality
of the members of the class; it was what he
called liberality, to listen to various views courteously, even if you couldn't accept them all or
make them agree.

The question had now reached Dr. Fahrenglohz, and the members, both liberal and narrow, prepared for something terrible. They
knew, in general, that he believed nothing that
they themselves did; how then could his own
ideas be anything but dreadful?

The doctor looked mildly from behind his
very convex glasses, and said:

" Jesus was a mystic. From the spiritual
plane on which he lived it was impossible
for him to descend. He could say only that
which he believed. Pure-minded and wholly
regardless of ordinary earthly interests, he could
not be a utilitarian, in the vulgar acceptation of
the word. What thought he, what thinks any
philosopher, of how his theories may affect the

world? It is his duty to discover the truth, help or hinder whomsoever it may, and to speak it as he understands it, not in such fragments as other people may comprehend it. What did Buddha and Brahma? They spoke, they gave forth that which originated with them."

"And what did it all amount to?" asked Squire Woodhouse. "Business don't amount to a row of pins among *their* followers, according to the *Missionary Herald*, and virtue is worse off yet."

The doctor smiled condescendingly. "'He that hath ears to hear, let him hear,' as *your* prophet says. Is virtue and good business always to be found with those who sit under the words of Jesus?"

"N-no," said the Squire, "and that's just what we're driving at. If the words are understood—and followed—men can't help being good and successful."

"And so there is all the more need of careful, prayerful study of the words," remarked Mr. Prymm.

There was general disappointment, among those who had yet to speak, at the lack of any startling heresy in the doctor's utterances. Builder Stott in particular had felt that he might have an opportunity of defending the faith which he so unhesitatingly accepted, at no matter what intellectual difficulties, by abusing some heterodox utterance of the doctor; but the doctor's statements had seemed to him to resemble either a sphere—and a hollow one—from which all projectiles would glance harmlessly, or mere thin air, in which there was nothing to aim at. So he could do nothing but assert his own orthodoxy.

" I believe everything that Jesus said was meant just as it was spoken," said he; " whether what we call common sense has got anything to do with it or not, is none of our business. Of course we can't live up to it all —we're born in sin and shapen in iniquity ;

our hearts are deceitful above all things and desperately wicked—but what we can't do, he did for us, by dying on the cross. *We* can never act according to his teachings—we'd go to the poor-house or into our coffins as soon as we attempted it. If we *could* do it, there wouldn't have been any need of an atonement."

"Then the atonement is an excuse for rascality, is it?" asked Captain Maile. The Captain's own house had been erected by Builder Stott, and many had been his complaints of features which had proved not in accordance with the spirit of the contract.

Leader Bates felt extremely uncomfortable ; he never had liked personalities, and hated them all the worse when they interfered with that heavenly feeling which was to him the principal object of all religious meetings. He made haste to call upon Mr. Alleman, and that gentleman replied :

"Mr. Leader, there can be no doubt that

this passage was spoken to living men, about living interests, and that it not only can be lived up to by the exercise of such qualities as men already have, but that it *must* be treated and respected as truth if men do not wish the disgrace and penalties of hypocrisy. Of what consequence is it to true righteousness if men will or will not reconcile scriptural injunctions with business desires? Bring business up to truth, not truth down to business, is the earthly application of Christ's teachings."

" That," said Builder Stott, " may be all right in running a first-class academy, but you can't run the building business on any such basis."

The hour for dismission was reached at that instant, with Mr. Hopper still nervously shaking the coat-tail pocket which contained the review with the article on the " True Location of the Holy Sepulchre." Two or three of the members departed, but the greater number stood about and discussed the discussion.

"Well, everybody had a chance to speak his mind," said Mr. President Lottson.

"That's so," said Mr. Buffle, founder of the class, rubbing his hands enthusiastically. "Nobody was afraid of his neighbor's opinions."

"There seemed a general disposition to view the subject from all points," remarked Mr. Prymm.

"Not much regard paid to evidence," said young Lawyer Scott, "but still an evident willingness to open the case fairly."

"There was not a proper interest displayed in the future location of the soul," complained Mr. Jodderel; "still the members acted like good listeners."

"There was a little too much talking back," said Mr. Radley; "men should be more careful about treading on each other's corns. But there was a real, liberal spirit shown throughout, and that's what religious societies need."

"Men shouldn't *have* corns, if they don't want them trodden on," said Captain Maile.

"I won't complain, though—I never saw so little narrowness in so large a religious gathering."

"I take great delight in recalling the conference we have had," said Dr. Fahrenglohz. "I supposed, when I heard of this association, that it would not bear the test of differences of opinions, but I am grateful for the respect shown to me, and pleased at the courtesy displayed toward others."

Squire Woodhouse waited until Mr. Alleman disappeared, and then burst into a small group exclaiming :

"Now, I like Alleman first rate—all of my children go to his academy—but I *do* wonder whether he could run a farm with those notions of his? I'm glad the class listened respectfully, though—it showed that nobody was afraid that a little liberality would hurt any one."

CHAPTER III.

THE members of the Scripture Club did not put off their holy interest with their Sunday garments, as people of the world do with most things religious. When the little steamboat *Oakleaf* started on her Monday morning trip for the city, the members of the Scripture Club might be identified by their neglect of the morning papers and their tendency to gather in small knots and engage in earnest conversation. In a corner behind the paddle-box, securely screened from wind and sun, sat Mr. Jodderel and Mr. Prymm, the latter adoring with much solemn verbosity the sacred word, and the former piling text upon text to demonstrate the final removal of all the righteous to a new state of material existence in a better ordered planet. In the one rocking-chair of the cabin sat insurance President Lottson, praising to Mr. Hopper, who leaned obsequiously upon the back of the chair and occasionally hopped vivaciously around it, the self-disregard of the disciples, and the evident inability of anyone within sight to follow their example. The prudent Waggett was interviewing Dr. Fahrenglotz, who was going to attend the meeting of a sort of Theosophic Society, composed almost entirely of Germans, and was endeavoring to learn what points there might be in the Doctor's belief which would make a man wiser unto salvation, while Captain Maile stood by, a critical listener, and distributed pitying glances between the two. Well forward, but to the rear of the general crowd, stood Deacon Bates in an attitude which might have seemed conservative were it not manifestly helpless, Mr. Buffle with the smile peculiar to the successful business man, Lawyer Scott, with the air of a man who had so much to say that time could not possibly suffice in which to tell it all, Squire Woodhouse, who was in search of a good market for hay, Principal Alleman, who was in chase of an overdue shipment of text-books, and Mr. Radley, who with indifferent success was filling the self-assigned roll of moderator of the little assemblage.

"Nothing settled by the meeting?" said Mr. Buffle, echoing a despondent suggestion by Deacon Bates. "Of course not. You don't suppose that what theologians have been squabbling over for two thousand years can be settled in a day, do you? We made a beginning and that's a good half of anything. Why, I and every other man that builds boats have been hard at work for years, looking for the best model, and we haven't settled the question yet. We're in earnest about it—we can't help but be, for there's money in it, and while we're waiting we do the next best thing—we use the best ones we know about."

"Don't you think you'd get at the model sooner, if some of you weren't pig-headed about your own, and too fond of abusing each other's?" asked Mr. Radley.

"Certainly," admitted Mr. Buffle, "and that's why I wanted us to get up a Bible-class like the one we have. If everybody will try to see what's good in his neighbors theories and what's bad in his own, his fortune—his religion, I mean—is a sure thing. Fiddling on one string always makes a thin sort of a tune."

"There were a good many small tunes begun yesterday, then," observed Squire Woodhouse.

"Well," said Mr. Buffle, "I thought something of the kind, myself, but a man can't break an old habit to pieces all at once. Things will be different before long, though."

"There is no reason why they shouldn't," said Principal Alleman, "excepting one reason that's stronger than any other. You can't get to the bottom of any of the sayings of Christ,

the Prophets or the Apostles without finding
that they mean, Do Right. And when you reach
that point, what is in the man and not what is
in the book comes into play, or, rather, it always should but seldom does."

"I suppose that's so," said Mr. Buffle, soberly.

"In and of ourselves we can do nothing,"
remarked Deacon Bates.

"It's very odd, then, that we should have
been told to do so much," replied Principal
Alleman.

"It was to teach us our dependence upon a
higher power," said Deacon Bates, with more
than his usual energy.

"Are we only to be taught, and never to
learn, then?" asked Principal Alleman. "Some
of my pupils seem to think so, but those who
depend least upon the teacher and act most
fully up to what they have been taught are the
ones I call my best scholars."

Deacon Bates's lower lip pushed up its
neighbor; in the school-room, the Principal's

theory might apply, but in religion it was different, or he (Deacon Bates) had always been mistaken, and this possibility was not to be thought of for an instant. Fortunately for his peace of mind, the boat touched her city dock just then, and from that hour until five in the afternoon, when he left his store for the boat, religious theories absented themselves entirely from Deacon Bates's mind.

The last meeting of the class was still the most popular subject of conversation among the members, however, and interest of such a degree could not help be contagious. Other residents of Valley Rest, overhearing some of the chats between the members, expressed a desire to listen to the discussions of the class, and to all was extended a hearty welcome, without regard to race, color, or previous condition of religious servitude, and all were invited to be doers as well as hearers. So at the next session appeared ex-Judge Cottaway, who had written a book and was a vestryman of St. Amos Parish, Broker Whilcher, who worshipped with the Unitarians but found them rather narrow, and Broker Whilcher's bookkeeper, who read Herbert Spencer, and could not tell what he himself believed, even if to escape the penalty of death. Various motives brought men from other churches, including even one from Father McGarry's flock, and all of them were assured that they might say whatever they chose, provided only that they believed it.

"Shall we continue our consideration of last Sunday's lesson?" asked Deacon Bates, after the opening prayer had been offered. "We have some new members, and should therefore have some additional views to consider."

"Let's hear everybody," said Captain Maile. "If we talk as long about this verse as we'll *have* to talk before we reach any agreement, we'll all die before we can reach the square up-and-down verses that are further along in this same sermon."

"If the class has no objection to offer, we

will continue our study of the third verse of the
fifth chapter of Matthew, and those who spoke
on last Sunday will allow the newer members
and others an opportunity to make their views
known." As Deacon Bates spoke, his eye
rested warningly on Mr. Jodderel.

" I think," said Mr. Jodderel, " that the new
members ought to know what ideas have already been presented, so as to throw any new
light upon them, if they can. The nature of
the kingdom of heaven, now, is the most
important question suggested by the lesson,
and——"

" It won't be of the slightest consequence to
anyone," interrupted Principal Alleman, " unless they first comply with the condition which
the verse imposes upon those who want to
reach the kingdom."

"I wouldn't be too sure of that," remarked
President Lottson, " while Jesus said that the
poor in spirit should have the kingdom of
heaven, He didn't say that no one else should

share it with them. What is written doesn't always express all that is meant."

"It doesn't in insurance policies, anyhow," said Squire Woodhouse, "when my barn burned——"

"Time is precious, my brethren," said Deacon Bates hastily, scenting a personality, "I will therefore ask Judge Cottaway for his opinion of the passage."

"I think," said the Judge, with that impressive cough which is the rightful indulgence of a man who has written a volume on the rules of evidence, "that 'poor in spirit' undoubtedly means unassuming, rightly satisfied with what is their due, mindful of the fact that human nature is so imperfect that whatever a man obtains is probably more than he deserves. They can not be the meek, for special allusion is made to the meek in this same group of specially designated persons. Neither can it refer to people who are usually called poor-spirited persons, to wit, those who are too devoid of what is commonly designated as spirit, for these are properly classified as peace-makers, and have a similar though not identical bless-ing promised to them."

" The class owes its thanks to the Judge for his clear definition of the term ' poor in spirit,' " said Mr. Jodderel, " and if he can be equally distinct upon the expression ' kingdom of heav-en' he will put an end to a great deal of sense-less blundering."

" I know of but one definition," said the Judge, " heaven is the abode of God and the angels, and of those who are finally saved."

" Ah, but *where* is it ? *that's* the question this class wants answered," said Mr. Jodderel, twisting his body and craning his head for-ward as he awaited the answer.

" Really," said the Judge, " you must excuse me.   I don't know where it is, and I can't see that study as to its locality can throw any light upon the lesson."

This opinion, delivered by an ex-Judge, who

had written a book on rules of evidence, would have quieted almost anyone else, and the members' faces expressed a sense of relief as they thought that Mr. Jodderel also would be quieted. But Mr. Jodderel was not one of the faint-hearted, and in his opinion faint-heartedness and quietness were one and the same thing.

"No light upon the lesson?" echoed Mr. Jodderel. "Why, what is the Bible for, if not to inform us of our destiny? What is this world but a place of preparation for another? And how can we prepare ourselves unless we know what our future place and duty is to be?"

"Next!" exclaimed Deacon Bates with more than his usual energy, and Mr. Jodderel sank back into his chair and talked angrily with every feature but his mouth, and with his whole body besides. "Mr. Whilcher has some new ideas to present, no doubt," continued the leader, bracing himself somewhat firmly in his chair, for the Deacon naturally expected an assault from a man of Mr. Whilcher's peculiar views.

"Poverty of spirit seems to me to be old English for modesty," said Mr. Whilcher, "We know very little, comparatively, of the great designs of God, and about as little of the intentions of our fellow-men, so we should be very careful how we question our maker or criticise our neighbors. No human being would appreciate divine perfection if he saw it; no man can give his fellow-men full credit for what they *would* do, if they were angels, and are sorry because they can't do. I think the passage means that only by that modesty, that self-repression, by which alone a man can accept the inevitable as decreed by God, and forbear that fault-finding which comes fully as easy as breathing, can a man be fitted for the companionship of the loving company which awaits us all in the next world."

"Whereabouts?" asked Mr. Jodderel.

Half-a-dozen members filibustered at once,

and Mr. Jodderel was temporarily suppressed, after which Squire Woodhouse remarked :

" Well, now, that sounds first rate—I never knew before that Unitarians had such good religion in them—no harm meant, you know, Whilcher."

" Now let us hear from Mr. Bungfloat," said Deacon Bates.

Mr. Bungfloat, bookkeeper to Mr. Whilcher, hopelessly explored his memory for something from Herbert Spencer that would bear upon the subject, but finding nothing at hand, he quoted some expressions from John Stuart Mills' essay on " Nature," and was hopelessly demoralized when he realized that they did not bear in the remotest manner upon the topic under consideration. Then Deacon Bates announced that the subject was open for general remark and comment. Mr. Jodderel was upon his feet in an instant, though the class has no rule compelling the members to rise while speaking.

" Mr. Leader," said he, " everybody has spoken, but nobody has settled the main question, which is, where is the 'kingdom of heaven?' Everybody knows who the poor in spirit are ; any one who didn't know when we began has now a lot of first class opinions to choose from. But where and what is heaven—*that* is what we want to know."

A subdued but general groan indicated the possibility that Mr. Jodderel was mistaken as to the desires of the class. Meanwhile, young Mr. Banty, who had been to Europe, and listened to much theological debate in cafés and beer-gardens, remarked.

" I'm not a member of this respected body, but I seem to be included in the chairman's invitation. I profess to be a man of the world —I've been around a good deal—and I never could see that the poor in spirit amounted to a row of pins. If they're fit for heaven they ought to be fit for something on this side of that undiscovered locality."

" Discovered millions upon millions of times, bless the Lord," interrupted Squire Woodhouse.

" Well, the discoverers sent no word back, at any rate," said young Mr. Banty, " so there's one view which I think ought to be considered; isn't it possible that Jesus was mistaken? "

Mr. Prymm turned pale and Deacon Bates shivered violently, while a low hum and a general shaking of heads showed the unpopularity of young Mr. Banty's idea.

" The class cannot entertain such a theory for an instant," answered Deacon Bates, as soon as he could recover his breath, " though it encourages the freest expression of opinion."

" Oh ! " remarked Mr. Banty, with a derisive smile. The tone in which this interjection was delivered put the class upon its spirit at once.

" Our leader means exactly what he says,"

said Mr. Jodderel; "any honest expression of opinion is welcome here."

"If such were not the case," said Mr. Prymm, "a rival class would not have been formed."

"And none of us would have learned how many sides there are to a great question," said Mr. Buffle.

"Larger liberty wouldn't be possible," said Builder Stott. "Why, I've just had to shudder once in awhile, but the speakers meant what they said, and I rejoiced that there was somewhere where they could say it."

"I've said everything *I've* wanted to," remarked Squire Woodhouse.

"That's so," exclaimed insurance President Lottson.

"I havn't seen any man put down," testified Captain Maile, "and I don't yet understand what to make of it."

"Nobody could ask a fairer show," declared Mr. Radley.

"The utmost courtesy has been displayed

toward me," said Dr. Fahrenglotz, "although I am conscious my views are somewhat at variance with those of others."

" The nature of proof has not been as clearly understood as it should have been," said young Lawyer Scott ; " but no one has lacked opportunity to express his sentiments."

" So far from fault being found with the freedom of speech," said Mr. Alleman, " the sentiment of the class is, I think, that the expression of additional individual impressions would have been cordially welcomed, as they will also hereafter be."

Young Mr. Banty felt himself to be utterly annihilated, and the pillars of the class looked more stable and enduring than ever, and felt greatly relieved when the session ended, and they could congratulate each other on the glorious spirit of liberty which had marked their collective deliberations. And when Squire Woodhouse dashed impetuously from the room, and returned to report that Dr. Humbletop's class consisted of one solitary pupil, several of the members unconsciously indulged in some hearty hand-shaking.

CHAPTER IV.

A SOLEMN HOUR COMPLETELY SPOILED.

THE Scripture Club of Valley Rest, on the fourth day of its assembling, found itself a fixed and famous institution. Some of the members had at first regretted that no one of the smaller rooms in the church edifice was unoccupied at the hour of session ; but this regret was soon abandoned, for the reason that neither the pastor's study nor the regular Bible class-room, had either been available at the noon-day hour, would have been large enough to accommodate the class and its visitors. The main audience-room was the only one which was adequate to the requirements of the class. When the benediction was pronounced after the morning sermon, a large portion of the congregation remained, and, instead of chatting leisurely with the occupants of neighboring pews and preventing the exit of unsociable people, they hurried to the seats nearest the corner occupied by the class. Even then, those who came last were occasionally compelled to exclaim " Louder!" for the attendants of the Second Church did not compose the entire body of hearers. Members of the five other churches in the town, though loath to depart from their denominational associations and pride so far as to worship elsewhere, were not only without scruples against listening to an informal body like the Scripture Club, but hurried from their own places of worship to the Second Church, and some of them were suspected even of staying away from their own services in order to reach the Scripture Club in time to secure good seats.

The effect of all this upon the Club was stimulating in high degree. Its first effect was to decrease whatever tendency to personality existed; whatever might be the week-day

opinions of the members about each other, on
Sunday every one tacitly agreed to the application of the Satanic rule that religion is religion, and business is business. Some special
effort was necessary to bring Squire Woodhouse to forget, for an hour in the week, his
burned barn and the action of President Lottson's insurance company; but finally the
Squire's pride closed his lips upon this tender
subject. Members, who before had possessed
no religious ideas excepting those they had
adopted at second-hand, now began to think for
themselves, and being men of natural wits well
sharpened by business experience, they speedily
developed theories of their own, and strengthened their own pet positions. The few religious
books of reference in the village library—many
of them having once been gladly given to the
library by the very men who now sought
them—were in demand at early morn and dewy
eve, pastors' libraries were ransacked, and some
members even consulted booksellers, and pur-

chased works bearing upon their own special lines of thought and belief. Respect for the ideas of others did not necessarily imply assent, so discussion was frequent and animated. Champions of the faith—as delivered unto themselves—were numerous, and assailants of the truth as held by the orthodox were in sufficient numbers to keep their antagonists from lapsing into a condition of mere assertion. And over and around everything, like a glorious halo, was the assurance, always prominent, that free speech would not only be welcomed, but that the lack of it, from any motive of fear or conservatism, would greatly be regretted by every member.

The discussion of the first beatitude consumed the time of four entire sessions, and during all these days it was in vain that Mr. Hopper carried the review containing the paper on "The True Location of the Holy Sepulchre." When, on the fifth day, Deacon Bates asked whether any other members had anything to say on the

subject under consideration, Captain Maile
made answer :

"Call it a drawn fight, and give it up at that ;
if any man here *had* been whipped, he wouldn't
know it."

"Oh, come, come!" said Squire Woodhouse,
"I'll join issue with you on that. *I* want to
know what 'poor in spirit' means, and have a
share in the kingdom of heaven———"

"But you don't want to know where or what
the kingdom is," interrupted Mr. Jodderel.

"Yes, I do ; but I want first to know what
poor in spirit means. I feel pretty sure about it
now, but———"

"That's it, exactly," said Captain Maile.
"But—but you don't want to be anything that
interferes with business. Give us something
easier, Mr. Leader."

There were some indignant whispers of dissent, but none of them were audible enough to
attract the attention of the class, and Deacon
Bates read the next verse.

"Blessed are they that mourn, for they shall be comforted," read Deacon Bates. "Brother Prymm, will you open the discussion of this beatitude?"

"There is none other more precious to the earthly nature," said Mr. Prymm, "and yet the passage proves the comprehensiveness peculiar to inspired words. Sin and perplexity are the lot of all mortals, and they bring trouble with them; but the single sorrow which raises man up to God, and brings God down to man, is mourning. It may be done from sinful causes —upon earth—but whatever the cause, the act itself shows us how near God is to us, and what are his sentiments usward. He knows from the greatness and purity of his own nature how intense this sentiment may be, and his sympathy shows itself so tenderly in no other way as by this promise, that he will come to his children and comfort them when they are in sorrow. What an evidence of the need of a God does this promise afford! Where else can we

5

turn for true comfort when in trouble? Earthly friends lack that knowledge of us from which alone true sympathy can come; the pleasure of the flesh can give us nothing better than temporary forgetfulness; but the divine sympathy is perfect in its knowledge, timely and appropriate in its expression, and incalculable in its force and endurance."

"I am glad to offer my weak testimony in support of the remarks of Brother Prymm," said Builder Stott, who came next in the order of rotation. "I have had my sad experiences in this world,—all of you have had yours, I suppose,—but it seems to me that mine have been peculiar. I've trusted men and been swindled by them. I've been abused for things that I never thought of doing. I've lost dear ones that left places that have never been filled and never can be, and I have found no one whose words could be more than a mockery—one that wasn't intended, of course, but that hurt just as badly as if it had. It has been only when on

my knees, or praying silently as I walked the
street, that I found a sympathizing friend.
There can be no doubt in *me* about what that
passage means—I know all about it by blessed
experience."

"So do I," said Mr. Buffle. "I've been what
men call fortunate in this world's affairs, but if
any one here thinks that money can buy ex-
emption from misery, I want to tell him that
he's greatly mistaken. I lost a child two or
three years ago—some of you remember her;
I'd have changed places with the cheapest work-
man in my shipyard—yes, the most miserable
beggar in the street—if by doing so I could
have brought her back again. But money
couldn't do it, and, as our friend Stott has just
remarked, the best of earthly friends couldn't
take the sting away. I can't say that God's
comfort came just when I most wanted it, but
God is good and wise; he sent it when he
thought best, and it was full of blessing when it
came. It doesn't heal wounds to be comforted

by Heaven—the wounds remain as tender as
ever ; but the pain and the feeling of hopeless-
ness depart, and a man is made to feel like the
wounded soldier, or the wrecked, starved sailor
when help comes—he *knows* he has a friend to
lean upon."

Mr. Buffle felt for his handkerchief and applied it to his eyes ; an operation which, in spite
of his great-heartedness, he seldom had occasion to perform in public : meanwhile Broker
Whilcher said :

" I don't agree with every one here, as most
of you know ; but the beautiful promise which
forms the subject of our lesson to-day has been
fulfilled to me. I can't explain how, but I profess to be too much of a man to deny what I
learn by experience, even when I can't ascertain
who my teacher is. My own great ups and
downs of life have been principally social, and,
as has been remarked by others, they are the
hardest of any to bear. And somehow—I wish
I *could* learn how—I have been helped, soothed,

sustained, whenever I could abandon myself to the influence of whatever higher power it is that looks to the hearts of men and sees that they are not entirely crushed."

"The older a man grows in years and experience," said Judge Cottaway, without his official cough, "the greater his experience of sorrow. The exercise of wisdom may prevent some troubles that carelessness and ignorance may induce, but even then there is more of misery in life than any human influences can avert. I believe, after much deliberation upon the evidence adduced from the affairs of men, that the Comforter is also the one who afflicts in many cases; but so certain am I of his wisdom and goodness that I would never avert his chastening hand. The cry of Christ in the garden, 'O, my Father, if it be possible, let this cup pass from me: nevertheless not as I will, but as thou wilt,' should be the sentiment of every one that is in affliction. That more bitter cry that was sounded from the Cross may also be, without sin, re-echoed by the human soul in trouble; but every one learns, by blessed experience, that the soul is never forsaken, and that our sorrows are known to Heaven better than they are to ourselves."

Mr. Jodderel sat next, and Squire Woodhouse whispered to his nearest neighbor:

" Too bad; he'll bring in the kingdom of heaven and pit it against the Ring." But to the astonishment of every one, Mr. Jodderel said only:

" No one knows more of this blessed Comforter than I. My childish days were heavily clouded; I was abused in youth; I am misunderstood now; I have lost dear ones; a long procession has preceded me to the grave, each member of it leaving my heart more lonely than before, and the time has come when I am too old to search for new friends and dear ones. But upon my knees, or as I commune with him upon my bed in the night season, or when I read his precious promises given by word of

mouth or through his holy prophets, I find con-
solation and hope and cheer, and forget that
I am a lonely old man in an unsympathetic
world."

"Captain Maile?" said Leader Bates, and
the ex-warrior responded :

"Everything I have heard this morning
agrees with my own experience, and no matter
what doubters may say and hypocrites may
help them to make people believe, I can
never forget the special blessings I have received in affliction, and when I have least expected them."

Squire Woodhouse sat next to Captain Maile,
and joined in the general acknowledgment by
saying :

"You all know me, my friends ; you know
I've often had a pretty hard row to hoe, for
often it's been in a shape that hoeing couldn't
help. But when the worst has come, and I
couldn't do anything but stand still and endure
it ; when I couldn't shake it off, or forget it, or

improve it any way, there came in just when I couldn't expect it, or see how it could happen even with God managing it; when every one I leaned on failed me, and I had to shut myself up in my own miserable heart—then there came a visitor that made himself at home, helped me, changed me, made a new man of me, and showed me that the worst chance of man is the best one for God—blessings on his holy name forever."

Then Dr. Fahrenglotz said:

"For myself, I have no family ties. I never knew my parents, for they entered into the unknowable while I was yet a babe; I have had neither brother nor sister, but I have had friends, and they have passed away, leaving my heart as empty as if it had never contained any other denizen. I have felt the last pulsation of the heart-dealings of many of you, and have watched you afterward with a solicitude which it might have seemed officious for me to have expressed. And to myself and to others I have known true, mysterious comfort to come, I know not from where; the great outer, the intangible envelope of the human heart, is hidden from my sight and thought; but from it I know there comes a subtle mystery whose influence transcends that of mortals, and which influence is tender, soothing, and lasting — an influence which I cannot characterize more aptly than to say that it must come from some one or some principle of nature akin to that of Him whom most religious bodies denominate The Great Physician."

"Excuse me, gentlemen," said young Mr. Banty, who had come in late, and had, sorely against his will, been compelled to occupy a seat among those whom he called "the Saints;" "Excuse me; I didn't come in to say anything to-day, but, things going as they are, I can't be quiet. I went abroad a year ago; most of you know why. There was a lady in the question. She died; I suppose it was best for her, for I didn't, in the slightest degree, begin to be fit for her, but her death didn't hurt me any the less. I haven't, since then, been as good a man as I should have been. I don't mind saying that the ways in which I've tried to forget my trouble haven't been such as have done me any good. But as everybody else has opened his heart to-day, I wouldn't be a bit of a man if I kept mine shut. I want to say that when I have a quiet hour, and get to thinking about that girl, there's something happens that I don't understand, but I'm very thankful for. I got to be a great deal less despairing, though, at the same time, I think a great deal more tenderly about *her*. `I lose my ugliness at losing her; I see how much better it was for *her*; I see how things had better go as they should than as *I* want them, and I come out of that time less willing to go on a spree, less anxious to see the boys, and more anxious to go on thinking than to do anything else."

The order of rotation demanded that the next

speaker should be Mr. Alleman, and that gentleman remarked:

"I am heartily glad to see that there is one
ground upon which all of us can meet. Those of
you who know me know what frequent occasion
I have had to learn all that you have learned of
the unspeakable power of a comforting God. I
have instinctively passed the greater portion of
my life in my affections, for I know of no other
sentiment which is so all-comprehensive ; and
through these I have found daily new causes
for mourning. We are informed by Jesus that
the greatest of all commandments is that enjoin-
ing love toward God, and that the second is like
unto it, 'Thou shalt love thy neighbor as thy-
self.' To try to fulfill this command is to have
constant incentives to mournfulness. Every
day I have them, from some cause heretofore
unexpected, and the causes involve so many
other people in troubles, which might be
avoided, and for which I can blame only myself,
that but for the presence of the Comforter I

would be driven to despair or madness. What a tremendous responsibility rests upon us, my friends, in this our greatest relation to humanity, and how impossible it would be to endure it unless aided by a power greater than our own. I cannot, by any words, express my satisfaction at hearing so many men, and, in other religious matters, men of such differing views, testify to the unfailing promptness of the Great Sympathizer. And I should be glad to hear a wider expression of experiences, and assure myself that, in troubles outside the range purely personal, my fellow-beings enjoy the comfort that I do. I am confident that the recital of such experiences would strengthen every one for greater works of humanity and love."

There was a dead silence for several minutes, and the leader finally relieved the uncomfortable sensation of the members by asking :

" Has any one any other remarks to offer?"

No one responded.

"The next lesson, which we will hardly have

time to begin to-day, will be upon the third beatitude," said Deacon Bates. "The class may consider itself dismissed, I suppose."

"Now, *wasn't* that just like Alleman?" asked Squire Woodhouse of Captain Maile. "We were having the most heavenly time I ever did know inside of a church, and he utterly ruined it."

"The rest of you didn't act a bit as if you'd ruined yourselves, did you?" asked the Captain, in reply.

"Why, how?" asked the Squire.

"Eyes have they, but they see not," answered the Captain, starting abruptly for his carriage.

CHAPTER V.

THE members of the club spent a whole week in trying to recover from the bad effects of Mr. Alleman's peculiar and untimely harangue, and even then they did not succeed.

"We were getting into such an unusual, such a heavenly state of mind," explained Mr. Hopper, "and the Lord knows that heavenly states of mind are scarce enough anywhere under the best of circumstances. We were forgetting all the tricks, the games that had been come upon us in the discussion of other points on which the brethren had made up their minds, and picked out their trees to hide behind; and we were having just the happy, quiet, sympathetic time which a man knows how to appreciate when he's knocked about the world for a little while, when all of a sudden Alleman must come in, and spring some of his peculiar notions upon us. I don't see why the Lord lets such men torment the world about religious affairs. They're good enough in every other way."

Other members of the class wondered also; and when, on the following Sunday, Deacon Bates asked if any one else had any remarks to make on the late lesson, nobody answered. So the leader read:

"'Blessed are the meek, for they shall inherit the earth.' Judge Cottaway"—the Deacon had skillfully inveigled the Judge into a front seat before the discussion began, so as to have a strong and respectable opening—"we would be glad to learn your views of this passage."

"I take it to mean," answered the Judge, "that meekness is a virtue so highly esteemed by the Almighty, that he offers, as an incentive to its cultivation, the most highly valued of earthly inducements. Meekness seems to be the antithesis, the exact opposite of strife, and so much of strife is so causeless and harmful, yet so attractive to the ordinary mind, that those who indulge in it are by this passage warned by implication. Meekness is not a virtue of such greatness as poverty of spirit, as may be inferred from the smaller reward promised to those' who practice it, and——"

"I want to correct the gentleman right there," exclaimed Mr. Jodderel. "What earth are they to inherit? *This* earth? Why, everybody laughs at that notion. A man's got to fight awfully hard to get anything in this world, and harder yet to keep whatever he gets. The path of meekness leads but to the poor-house. The earth alluded to evidently means the new earth, which, in the Revelation, John beheld, in connection with the new heaven. That new earth appeared after the destruction of the old one; and for what could it have appeared but to be populated by the redeemed spirits from this? *That* was the kingdom of heaven, and the text before us evidently refers to it. 'The meek shall inherit the earth;' the apostles, to whom this passage was spoken, needed no more definite expression about the matter, of which the Master doubtless had spoken many times with them. The whole passage seems to me an exact repetition of the one before it, just to give emphasis to the first."

"I wonder if that's exactly straight?" remarked Squire Woodhouse, more with the air of a man in a soliloquy than one asking a question. "If there *is* a way of inheriting the earth, or even a little piece of it, I'd like to know all about it; but if it's only the next world that the passage refers to——"

"If it refers only to the next world, you're not in such a hurry to understand it," interrupted Captain Maile.

"We—ell," drawled the Squire, "that isn't exactly the way I was going to finish off, but I guess it's pretty near the truth. It *don't* sound well either, does it?"

"Brother Prymm?" said Deacon Bates, and

6

the champion of orthodoxy responded to the invitation by saying,

"The meek are undoubtedly those who follow the non-resistant injunctions which are found everywhere in the New Testament; they are the men who when one cheek is struck turn the other also, who render not railing for railing."

"And who, when the coat is taken, will offer the cloak also," added Captain Maile.

"Certainly," said Mr. Prymm, with rather a wry face, "though I cannot, with any present light, see how the latter course would be practical and judicious. The other injunctions are but amplifications of the inspired saying, 'A soft answer turneth away wrath,' but how property rights can be maintained at all, if the injunction quoted by Captain Maile were followed, I am unable to see."

"It wouldn't work in the steamboat business," declared Mr. Buffle. "It's hard enough to get the worth of your money, even when men promise to pay; but if a man were to understand that by stealing one of my tug-boats he would have a right to expect a first-class lake packet as a present, I'd have to go out of business within a fortnight."

"I'm inclined to think the passage in question must be an interpolation by one of Christ's reporters," said President Lottson, who had been taking a cautious course of Matthew Arnold.

"Why, if *I* were to live up to that injunction," said Builder Stott, "folks would want to modify their house plans every day. In fact they do it now. The moment I try to oblige a man by giving a little more than his contract calls for, he wants something else. Women in particular are perfectly awful that way; they——"

"Ladies are present," remarked Lawyer Scott, who was considerable of a ladies' man.

"Just think of a broker trying to do business in that way!" exclaimed Broker Whilcher.

"Or a man whose principal crop is hay," said Squire Woodhouse.

"Or an importer of English cutlery," suggested Mr. Jodderel. "Still, the passage ought either to be explained away or lived up to, for if going contrary to business rules is necessary to inherit the new earth—it's contrary to sense that *this* earth can be got hold of by any such unbusiness-like operation—the new earth, otherwise the kingdom of heaven——"

"Members will please bear in mind the rule that remarks are to be made in regular order," interposed the leader hastily. "We will hear from Brother Hopper."

"I suppose meekness means patience," said the gentleman addressed, nervously clutching his coat-tail pocket with its precious contents; "not getting into a stew about everything, in fact; but how a man is to be so, when everything goes on the way it shouldn't, is more than *I* can tell, and how they're going to get the earth for their pains is a bigger puzzle yet."

Mr. Lottson being called upon, said:

" I can only repeat about this passage my remarks upon the one which preceded it. It means exactly what it says, but it means it only in a spiritual sense, and only to those to whom it was said—to the disciples of Christ, and those whose conditions of life are equally admirable and peculiar. The disciples were meek—all but Peter, that is—and *he* stopped being a man of the world after he learned that he couldn't be that and a consistent disciple too. And look at the result! Haven't the disciples of Christ inherited the earth? Hasn't the blood of the martyrs been the seed of the Church? Hasn't the non-resistent, patient, self-sacrificing course of Christian missionaries led to the conversion of powerful heathen nations, opened avenues of trade between them and Christian countries——"

" Which have straightway been traveled over by men who rob the heathen, poison them with rum, and kill them off with the popular vices of civilization," interrupted Captain Maile.

" Opened avenues of trade between them and Christian countries," resumed President Lottson, as if no interruption had occurred, "created a demand for the Bible and the school, discouraged war, extended the area of production, established representative governments in the place of irresponsible despotisms, brought from foreign lands, to study our institutions, men whose fathers and grandfathers were brutal savages, and hastened the coming of the day when at the name of Jesus every knee shall bend and every tongue confess him Lord? Business alone could never have done this; it required a special development of mind, and to those whom he had created for this purpose Jesus enounced this promise, which was the only one that in the nature of things could be made to them about earthly interests."

"I declare!" whispered Squire Woodhouse to Mr. Buffle, "Lottson did that splendidly. If it wasn't for the way he treated me about that barn I should say that Lottson ought to have gone into the ministry." At the same moment Deacon Bates called Mr. Prymm to the chair, took the floor himself, and said :

" There was a remark dropped by Mr. Lottson, and followed up in his excellent speech, which I am certain conceals a truth which is not clearly enough realized. If it was, a number of puzzling questions that have been before the class could have easily been answered. He said the passage should be taken in a spiritual sense. It certainly should. God is a Spirit; our own spirits are our only immortal parts; everything else in us and everything around us is transient and perishable. The meek should be meek in a spiritual way; they should not be puffed up with knowledge, or what they think to be such, but should in humility open their hearts to the influences of the Holy Spirit. Business has nothing to do with our eternal welfare; it is only one of the necessary but transient affairs of our perishable, material bodies; but the things unseen are eternal. If we would constantly keep this fact in our minds I am sure many of our present difficulties in studying the Scriptures would disappear. This earth is not our abiding place; our time here is but short; 'A thousand years are but as a day in His sight;' heaven is our final and eternal home, and it was to instruct us how to prepare our souls for the future state of existence that the prophets spoke and Jesus came to earth."

"According to that, it don't matter how we do business," said Squire Woodhouse; "every man can be just as sharp and underhanded as he pleases. Well, it's a comfortable belief, but I think you're mistaken, Deacon, about its being lost sight of; I think pretty much everybody lives up to it, as far as business goes."

"Dr. Fahrenglotz," remarked the leader, in evident confusion at the moral deduced from his theory.

"Although not attaching to the words that degree of authority that some do," said the Doctor, "their unselfish tendency and their moral beauty convince me that they have an important meaning. That they can apply to the common affairs of life I cannot believe, for the theory is contrary to reason and experience. They probably refer to some coming state of society when the application of true reason shall have raised men above their present physical and moral level, and enabled them to translate the mystic sayings of the world's great seers."

"Then the passage doesn't command anything that's really essential to salvation?" asked young Mr. Waggett.

"Oh, no, certainly not," said Captain Maile. "Nothing does, or if it does, our business is to get around it somehow, and look at some other side of it."

The leader called upon Mr. Alleman, who said :

"The simple fact that this saying was given is sufficient excuse and command to follow it, no matter what it brings us or takes from us. As, however, the material bearing of the pas-

sage has attracted more attention to-day than
the manifest desire of Christ, I wish to recall to
notice the peculiar wording. Jesus does not
say that the meek shall earn or acquire the
earth, but that they shall inherit it. An inheri-
tance is something that the child obtains from
the parent through love and affection. The
passage means : ' Be meek, not given to strife, not
stirring up wrath, attending to your own affairs,
not assuming to be better or more deserving
than others ; ' and God, who owns the earth and
all that is in it, who makes man his steward,
who pulleth down one and setteth up another,
who knows the uses of property better than we
do, and who sooner or later puts it into proper
hands, will *give* you the earth. Be meek, and
trust to God for appreciation, even upon
earth."

"One o'clock," observed President Lottson,
and the session closed.

"Now *wasn't* that just like Alleman ? " asked
Squire Woodhouse of Mr. Jodderel. " Beauti-

ful idea—perfectly heavenly; but nothing in it that a man can take hold of without running the risk of losing some of his property. He'd better not talk that way before the city booksellers, if he don't want to have to pay cash for every bill of books he buys."

And Captain Maile walked out singing to himself, but in a tone loud enough to be offensive, the old song beginning,

" Whip the devil around the stump."

CHAPTER VI.

BUILDER STOTT SAVES THE FAITH.

THE Scripture Club proceeded promptly to work on the ensuing Sunday. Too many men had brought to the previous meeting ideas which they could not find time to express; so on the second Sunday in which the nature and reward of the meek were considered, the members who had not expressed their views, with several who had, made haste to occupy front seats, so as to be sure of opportunities to speak.

Among these was Squire Woodhouse. He had several times ruined the regularity of the proceedings of other meetings, but still he was unsatisfied. He had not expressed his own views in full, partly because he had not been asked to do so, but principally because he had had no settled views to express. Now, how-

ever, the case was different.   He had leisurely
pondered over everything that he had heard in
the class, he had admired each original idea
with the true American heartiness toward new
notions, he had endeavored to reconcile them
with his unformulated but still very positive pre-
conceived religious opinions, and his honesty
had finally triumphed over his theology and his
sophistry.   When he came to church, therefore,
he neglected his own pew and took the front
seat and the extreme right end thereof, so when
Deacon Bates opened the exercises of the class
immediately after service, it was impossible not
to call upon Squire Woodhouse first of all.   The
Squire cleared his throat, waved his head about
in a dissatisfied manner, and finally said :

"This thing of being meek grows pretty
big when you think about it for a little while,
and the worst of it is that everything else in the
chapter is only a chip out of the same block.
All of it—being meek and everything else—
seems to come in the end to just this : you

mustn't be like folks in general, particularly like business men. I confess that I don't know exactly how to do it all, but it seems to me it must be done ˏby any one who believes that Jesus Christ had the right to say all that he did. I *don't* know how to be meek about the way I was swindled—treated, I mean—by the insurance companies when my barn burned down——"

" Personal!" whispered Mr. Prymm.

" I don't care if it *is* personal," said Squire Woodhouse. " I'm trying to point a moral, and it isn't my fault if other folks get in the way and get hurt. I don't know how to be meek when I'm abused, but——"

" It isn't required of you," said Mr. Jodderel. " You're expected to take care of what has been intrusted to you in your capacity as a steward of the Lord."

Many were the affirmative shakes of head which followed this remark.

" I suppose I am," said the Squire, " and so

long as I am a human being I won't be likely
to forget it; but whether when I get mad over
being swindled the anger all comes from my
feeling of being deprived of the Lord's property, I'm not so sure: I've a suspicion that
more of it comes from the heart of Squire
Woodhouse than from the kingdom of heaven."

"Not a bit of it," said Mr. Hopper, finding
at last a subject upon which he could speak
from the abundance of his heart. "Aren't you
working for the good of your family, and don't
St. Paul say that the man who don't look out
for his family is worse than an infidel?"

"Yes," said the Squire meditatively; "but
he don't tell you to boil over when there's
nothing to be gained by it, and when getting
mad makes you uninteresting to everybody, not
excepting yourself. He doesn't tell you to let
your suspicions manage your wits, and deter-
mine what sort of a man your neighbor is. The
man who gets the best of me in a trade may be
a scoundrel; I've always made it a rule to think

so, in fact; but when I come to think of it, I remember that I've sometimes made a hard, sharp trade myself without meaning anything wrong."

"You never carried back the unfair gains, though, when you saw what you'd done, did you?" asked Captain Maile.

"Well, no; not that I can recollect. I *have* tried to make it up to the man in some way or other, though."

"Taking pains to tell him why you were trying to do it?" asked the Captain.

"No—no, I can't say that I did—I don't know that I ever succeeded in doing it, any how," said the Squire honestly. "I'd think it over, off and on, and before I'd know it, the whole thing would fall out of my mind."

"So all you did was to ease your conscience —sing it to sleep, so to speak," continued the Captain. "You gave him all the good feeling you could, which you couldn't help giving any way, because you're naturally a good-hearted fellow, and then when you'd comforted yourself your work stopped."

"That's about the truth of the matter," replied the Squire, "though I didn't mean to out with it all so plainly before folks."

"Then," asked the Captain, "what's the moral difference between you and a rascal?"

"Sh—h—h—h" arose in chorus, even President Lottson taking part in the remonstrance.

"There isn't any," said the Squire stoutly, "if everybody's a rascal that's called one. But anybody that has the honest feelings *I* have, and that loves the square thing so much, and likes so much to see it done, *isn't* a rascal, and as I've had the kind of experiences I've told about, I don't see why other men that have had others like them, and that are called ugly names by me as well as everybody else, mayn't be just as right at heart as I am. After this I'm going to believe them so, any how."

There was a general nod of assent, and President Lottson arose, went around to where the

Squire was sitting, and offered his hand to the loser of the barn. The Squire took it, rather gingerly at first, but finally gave it a squeeze so hearty that President Lottson winced and drew his hand away.

"There!" exclaimed Captain Maile; "everything is all right now, of course. Goodness don't consist in doing right, but only in feeling right. Not what you do, but what you believe is what saves a man."

"Such is the decree of God and the decision of the Church," remarked Mr. Prymm.

"Then what saints the devils must be!" observed the Captain; "for *they* believe, though, to be sure, they tremble."

Another murmur of dissent was heard, and young Mr. Waggett hastened to throw a small quantity of oil on the troubled waters by remarking that whatever was sufficient to salvation was the fulfillment of God's plan as revealed in the holy Scriptures.

"I'm not through yet," said the Squire. "I

was coming to that point. Of course, other men make blunders very much like mine. I ought to be meek about judging them—I ought to forgive them their trespasses as I hope to have mine forgiven. But if there's so much excuse to think bad of men for what they do and don't do, we ought to put the cause out of the way, as well as to be patient with others as we'd have them patient with us. If I've had reason so many times to think the worst about church members, I suppose that sinners—sinners outside of the Church—must see them to be just as bad as I do. And if they do, what inducement is there for sinners to come into the Church?"

"Salvation!" promptly answered young Mr. Waggett.

"That's no moral inducement," said the Squire; "it's a selfish one."

"Oh, oh, oh!" exclaimed Builder Stott, supported by a sympathetic sensation which was manifested by most of the members, while Mr.

Jodderel sprang to his feet and said—shouted, almost:

"Mr. Chairman, I protest against this drifting away from the subject by talking all sorts of new-fangled notions that——"

"Free speech is the rule of this class," said Captain Maile. "*You've* given us a great deal about the kingdom of heaven that nobody ever heard of before, that's as unheard of in the Bible or the Church——"

"It *is* in the Bible," said Mr. Jodderel; "you'll find it in the prophets and apostles from beginning to end."

"I would suggest," said Mr. Prymm, in the most measured and soothing of tones, "that Brother Woodhouse should remember that we have but a single hour in the week to talk upon these subjects, and that however deeply he may be interested in his own peculiar views, it would be well to let all who are present have an opportunity to offer their views."

"Yes, let's get away from morality as soon as

we can," said Captain Maile.   "What's Sunday good for, if you can't in it get away from these enraging affairs of the week?   Nine-tenths of the moral questions in the world are started by business ; and who has any right to drag business into the Lord's house on Sunday, and just after a sermon, too?"

Faces confused, awry, angry, and merry, showed that the Captain had aroused a great deal of feeling, which, in sentiment, was not a unit.   Deacon Bates would have ordered the immediate relief of the class from extraneous subjects; but he had, from the beginning of the services, groaned over the fact that next to Squire Woodhouse sat Mr. Jodderel, and no one else could be called upon without destroying that rule of rotation upon which the leader generally depended for relief.   Silently resolving to pack the front seats on the succeeding Sunday, he said, in tones so subdued as to be almost pathetic :

"Brother Jodderel."

The members looked resignedly into each other's eyes; Mr. Stott turned to the table of Hebrew weights and measures in his Bible, and tried to lose himself in them; Broker Whilcher began slyly ciphering on a card, doubtless to solve some problem of the market; Mr. Alleman buried himself in a school report from some other town; Mr. Hopper re-read to himself the paper on "The True Location of the Holy Sepulchre;" and Mr. Buffle dropped into gentle slumber.

"I want to say," said Mr. Jodderel, "that you can't rightly know how to be meek until you know what's to be required of you in the earth which the meek are to inherit, and you can't know that without knowing where and what that earth is. Now, it *can't* mean this earth, for if the meek inherited it, it would be stolen away from them precious quickly. What happens to a meek man when somebody hits him without knocking the meekness out of him? —he gets hit again. What happens to him if somebody tries to swindle him out of his property, and he don't show that he won't endure imposition ?—he'll be cheated out of every cent. So the meekness that *we* think about is evidently not the thing for the earth that's to be inherited, · and the question is, what is?   And that brings us back to the question, What sort of a land are we going to inherit?   It——"

"If it is to be the abode of the finally saved and redeemed," said Mr. Radley, "I really don't see that meekness can be enjoined upon its inhabitants, unless we are all mistaken about the nature of the change that will take place after death.   Our mental condition will be determined for us, and we can't do better on this earth than act according to what seems the highest order of goodness.   I should really like to ask the gentleman if the next world is all that we are to think of while we remain in this one, and whether we are not to guide ourselves somewhat by the rights of other people as well as by our own desires?"

"This earth is not our abiding place," quoted Mr. Prymm; "we have a home not made with hands, eternal in the heavens."

"Certainly," said Mr. Jodderel; "that's correct; it *is* in the heavens—in the sky—the air above us, in which are suspended all the planetary bodies, one of which——"

"The gentleman has lost sight of my question," said Mr. Radley.

"So will everybody else," remarked Captain Maile. "If you press that question, you'll ruin the interest of this meeting. We didn't come here to learn what we ought to do; we're here to study out what's to be done for us."

"Not a bit of it," said Mr. Buffle, who has slowly awakened from his nap. "*I'm* not, any way. I'm as fond as any one else of getting anything; but I've already been blessed with more than I deserve, and I want to know what God's will concerning me is on earth as well as in heaven."

" Always providing it don't cost you anything," said Captain Maile.

" Nonsense," replied Mr. Buffle, rather angrily.
" I never refused to spend money on any really
useful charity."

Several members softly responded, " That's
true."

" Yes," said Captain Maile ; " you occasionally spend a penny out of a dollar, so to speak,
and you deserve credit for it, for very few other
men of means go so far ; you're ahead of your
day and generation. When I carry around a
subscription paper for anything, your name always has a handsome sum after it. But do you
really mean that you are going through this
Sermon on the Mount—if we live long enough
to get through it, which is very unlikely at the
present rate of progress—and practically agree
to what it says ? "

Mr. Buffle was cornered ; but blessed be
corners ! There are no other positions in life
from which a man can obtain so good a view of

5*

himself. Mr. Buffle studied the back of the seat in front of him for a few seconds ; looked rather blank, then very modest, then very manly, raised his head, and said : ·

" Yes, I do."

" Good ! " was the only word Captain Maile uttered, while Mr. Jodderel shook his head dismally, and exclaimed :

" Here we are, away from the subject again, Mr. Leader ! "

" We can hurry back to it, if the gentleman will answer my question," observed Mr. Radley.

" It's one o'clock," remarked Builder Stott.

The members arose, and most of them departed as soon as possible, while President Lottson turned to Stott, and said :

" You did that just in time."

" Well," said Stott modestly, " something had to be done. This old fight between faith and works has played the mischief wherever it's come up among men, and I'm not going to sit still and see it break up an interesting class like this.

I've no other chance to study the Bible except here, and I'm not going to have it ruined by a lot of theorists getting into a row.   I'm afraid it's too late, though.   Buffle got some new notion into his head when Maile cornered him there ; and he never lets go of any thought that strikes him as good.   The first thing you'll hear of will be another subscription list, with his name at the head, and he'll go into it with all his might, like he did about the building of this church ; and everybody will be worried by him, and he'll drag it in here, and act as if the Bible wasn't anything but a code of every-day morals."

"And forget all about the gospel-plan of salvation," said young Mr. Waggett.

"And the kingdom of heaven," suggested Mr. Jodderel.

"And the atonement, the central truth of the Scriptures," remarked Mr. Prymm ; "the vicarious efficacy of the atonement."

"And you'll shut your ears and eyes for fear

you might be converted and healed," said Captain Maile.

And the lingerers went straightway every man to his own house.

CHAPTER VII.

FREE SPEECH BECOMES ANNOYING.

AS the next meeting of the Scripture Club was about to open, certain members noticed that Mr. Jodderel had taken a seat which would entitle him to be the first person called upon for an opinion, and that he was divesting his pockets of a large number of books, most of them in faded and unconventional bindings. The members glanced at each other in terror, and when the opening prayer was concluded, Mr. Radley promptly exclaimed:

"Mr. Leader, the New Testament contains eight thousand verses, lacking two. With occasional quadrennial exceptions, there are but fifty-two Sundays in a year. We have already consumed, on an average, two Sundays to a verse ; at this rate we will need more than three hundred years to get through the New Testament.   Certain chapters, like the first chapter of Matthew and the third chapter of Luke, may form exceptions ; but as no man here can expect to live through much more than one-tenth of the time necessary to consider all the Gospels and Epistles, and as, even at the rate of a verse to a day, we would need to have our lives extended to several times the average longevity of mortals, I move that no single verse of Scripture shall be allowed to monopolize the attention of this class for more than one Sunday."

" I second the motion," said Mr. Alleman.

" Mr. Leader!" exclaimed Mr. Jodderel, " I object. We have spent two Sundays in considering the third beatitude, and we know no more about the whereabouts of the kingdom of heaven than when we began. If the proposed resolution takes effect now, and we find each verse of the Gospel as interesting as those already studied, no one knows how many of us may go from our deathbeds to the bar of God without knowing what to expect thereafter."

" And as God is only our Father, and the maker of the universe, and as we profess only to believe that he is wiser and more loving than any earthly parent, we daren't trust him to make the matter plain in the next world," observed Captain Maile.

" Question!" exclaimed every one who had perceived Mr. Jodderel's collection of books.

The question was put and carried, with but two dissenting voices, that of young Mr. Waggett being one of them.   Then the Leader read the verse :

" Blessed are they which do hunger and thirst after righteousness, for they shall be filled ;" and he asked Mr. Jodderel to open the discussion.   The gentleman addressed maintained a sulky silence for about two minutes, and finally remarked :

" This class seems bound to drift from spirit-

ual interests to temporal ones. The discussion
of the most important question suggested by
revelation has been prevented by an almost
unanimous vote, and now we are expected to
consider righteousness—mere morality—and its
rather dubious earthly reward. Filled? Why,
certainly they will be filled. In this late day
and age no man studies the moral law without
learning more than his mind can hold. Righteousness is good; it is necessary; men need to
learn about it, and others need to teach it, but
it's an awful come-down for the great fact of a
life beyond the grave."

"Certainly," said Captain Maile. "Righteousness is full of annoying little bothers about
what ought to be done for other people, while
the kingdom of heaven consists only of what is
to be done for ourselves. The Bible is crammed
full of these tormenting hints, and they always
appear just when a man would rather think
about something else; being given by divine
command, though, as the majority of the class

believe they are, I suppose they must be talked about in one way or another."

"They certainly should," said Broker Whilcher, who had been attracted to Mr. Jodderel's side by the array of books which that gentleman had begun to bring into line. "I have a sad reputation in point of orthodoxy, but what Captain Maile admits in sarcasm, *I* declare in the most solemn earnest. Morality is the order of things, and to a sinner like me, it seems to be a matter of prime importance. The interest which some of the members display in the nature of the kingdom of heaven is quite natural and proper; but how they propose to get there without morality, or, if they please, righteousness, is a puzzle to any man who reads the Bible and notices the importance attached to right conduct."

Deacon Bates promptly called President Lottson to the chair, took the floor himself, during an animated buzz by the class, and delivered with rapidity and emphasis the following speech:

"The method of reaching the better world, other than that of mere right doing, is rightly a matter of wonder to those who do not accept the inspired Word as a divinely designed and revealed plan for the salvation of sinful man. But if any of the good Book has binding force, all of it has; it stands or falls as a whole. We are informed by the apostle whose writings fill half of the New Testament, that 'The law of the Spirit of life in Christ Jesus hath made me free from the law of sin, which is death. For what the law'—that is, the law of righteousness—'for what the law could not do, in that it was weak through the flesh, God, sending his own Son in the likeness of sinful flesh, and for sin, condemned the flesh: that the righteousness of the law might be fulfilled in us, who walk not after the flesh, but after the Spirit.' And again we are told—oh, blessed assurance to those who find the law of righteousness impossible to fulfill!—that 'Abraham believed God, and it was imputed unto him for righteousness.' And we are also told, by the Saviour himself, that 'God so loved the world that he gave his only begotten Son, that whoso believeth in him shall not perish but have eternal life.' The law cannot be fulfilled by man ; we are all imperfect ; even when we will to do right the flesh wars against the spirit, and ignorance hinders men of the best intentions from doing what they would do. No man can be saved through the law ; excepting Jesus Christ, 'there is no other name under heaven whereby mankind can be saved.' I hope I have answered the gentleman's question in a manner distinct enough to be understood by him and such others here present to whom the Gospel plan of salvation is not as plain as it should be."

Deacon Bates resumed the chair, and Broker Whilcher replied :

" The explanation is perfectly satisfactory, as an answer to my question ; but it seems to me rather strange that any one should be willing to enter without effort when everybody is plainly told the desires of the king and benefactor whom they expect to meet."

Builder Stott sat next, and hastened to the rescue of faith from a freethinker like Mr. Whilcher.

"Suppose we do right always," said he, "what does it amount to? Our righteousness is as filthy rags in His sight, according to the inspired Word, and there's very little to hope for from anything so worthless. Nobody knows, even when he's doing his best, whether he is right or wrong. Even Satan sometimes appears as an angel of light. I can remember many a time when I've done what seemed to be exactly the right thing, and I not only went without any credit for it, but it seemed to make everything else go wrong. I begin to think the Lord knows his own business best, and that we can't meddle with it without getting into trouble."

"Getting into trouble is an excuse for not trying to do right, is it?" asked Captain Maile.

" No, it isn't," replied Mr. Stott quite testily ; " but a man can do a great deal of trying without succeeding, and without finding what is the proper thing to do. If we always knew just what was right, we should never get into trouble."

" I should like to ask the gentleman if Christ, the apostles, and prophets never got into trouble ? " said Mr. Alleman.

" I suppose they did," replied Mr. Stott, in visible embarrassment; " but—but that was divinely ordained for the benefit of sinful man."

" I should like also to ask if the gentleman considers the servant above his master, and free from responsibility for his conduct ? "

" No, of course not," said Mr. Stott, " but——"

Mr. Stott's expression remained unfinished for so long a time that Mr. Buffle took pity upon him, and remarked :

" It seems to me that unless hungering and thirsting after righteousness is a special virtue, it would not have been brought into this small group of qualities for which special blessings are promised.   If it is of so much consequence, we ought, in gratitude to God, to be anxious to learn just what righteousness is.   What we are to get for practicing it isn't of so much consequence.   And as there aren't many of us who have had so much reason to study the meaning of the word as our friend Judge Cottaway has, I think the class will be willing to waive the regular order of answering for once, and hear from the Judge his opinion of this important word."

Every one looked at the Judge, and Deacon Bates remarked that he would assume that Mr. Buffle expressed the sentiments of every one.

" Righteousness," said the Judge, with his regulation court-room air, " has but one meaning.   Philologically, legally, morally, and spiritually it means right doing.   Legally, righteousness consists in obeying the law, and, by implication, refraining from offending the law.   Morally, it is the very highest attainment possible to man ; in its fulfillment every ordinary duty of man toward man is accomplished. Spiritually, either under the old dispensation or the new, its range of application is increased and its nature strengthened and elevated. By no correct line of reasoning, nor by any honest interpretation of the letter and spirit of the Scriptures, can the imperative obligation of man to do righteousness be set aside. Because the term is frequently used as a synonym for piety, there is no excuse for substituting religious belief for it, for true piety must include righteousness, and has no foundation without it. The religious sentiment may suddenly take possession of a man who has previously been unrighteous; but it is reputable and valuable only so far as it induces its subject to attain, not only to negative righteousness, the refraining from misconduct, which the law holds to be sufficient, but also to that positive, active virtue, enjoined by all the inspired teachers, which shall make a man actively virtuous, and from higher motives than that of merely escaping penalties and gaining rewards.   Christ himself said of the moral law that every jot and tittle of it should be fulfilled."

"And it *was* fulfilled, on the Cross, when he cried, 'It is finished,'" interrupted Builder Stott.

"That's so," said young Mr. Waggett, now thoroughly aroused. "If it hadn't been, we never could have been saved."

"If the gentlemen really infer from Christ's last words that he meant to set aside the moral law," resumed Judge Cottaway, "the Church has been making a sad blunder during the twenty centuries which have followed the scene on Calvary.   During all these years, she has been a teacher of morality ; she has restrained, sometimes by persuasion, oftener by authority, sometimes by mistaken methods, sometimes in too lukewarm a manner, the baser passions of mankind, and encouraged the nobler qualities. In legal righteousness, the ancient Romans surpassed the world, and gave the models of all codes in operation to-day in the civilized world. And yet righteousness among the Romans, while wise, was often vindictive, and always wholly selfish.   The smallest, most ignorant community in our neighborhood to-day has a higher, purer conception and practice of morality than the central city of the world had in the time of Christ, and though it is not under the special direction of the Church, its growth can be traced back to no other source."

" I've often heard," said Mr. Jodderel, " that so an Episcopalian admits the authority and divine origin of his Church, he can believe anything he pleases, and the address we have just listened to convinces me that the statement is true. Why, gentlemen, while nobody has a higher respect for Judge Cottaway's character and attainments than I have, it seems to me that he isn't much different from a Unitarian or any other freethinker that imagines he has some hold upon religion. Why, gentlemen, what's

6

the good of Christ having lived and died at all, if we're still in bondage under the law? I don't mean that we're not to do right when we can— I want to do right as much as any man ever did—but if I've got to be bothered about all the little points that the Scribes and Pharisees fussed over, I don't see how much better off I am than they were."

" The gentleman is better off, as he expresses it," said the Judge, " because he has the benefit of the clearer light which Christ shed upon the law, and because through the life and death of Christ he has incentives to that love for the Source of all goodness which enables a man to overcome difficulties which, to the merely self-ish moralist, are utterly insurmountable. It is thus that love becomes the fulfillment of the law, for it enables the weakest man to overcome his worst inclinations."

" What becomes, then, of the doctrine of jus-tification by faith—the corner-stone of all Prot-estantism? " asked President Lottson.

"It remains as strong as ever," answered the Judge. "All are forgiven, our misdeeds committed in ignorance, when—mark the condition—when we are honest in intention and effort. 'The just'—the righteous, that is, those who do right to the best of their knowledge—'shall live by faith.' I would remind the gentleman that Christian theology, of every school, is based principally upon the principles laid down by that masterly jurist, the Apostle Paul, and that he makes of faith not the master but the subordinate of love. 'And now abideth faith, hope, love, these three; but the greatest of these is love.'"

"You can't go back on Paul," remarked Squire Woodhouse, "but it's often seemed to me that religious people treat Paul a great deal as the boys treat my orchard; they steal the apples they like the looks of best, but the best I've got are really the least handsome, and I generally have the full crop to myself."

Some one reminded the Leader that it was one o'clock, and the class arose.

"I'm going into Humbletop's class after this," said Builder Stott to President Lottson. "I was a little doubtful when this class was started whether it wouldn't sooner or later run things into the ground, and now it *has* done it. Cottaway is a dangerous man, for all his knowledge and squareness. There are men here, members of our Church, that'll be as likely as not to swallow all that he said, and then what'll their faith amount to? I say that if any such nonsense gets a hold in this church it ought to be made a matter of discipline."

"I think *I* shall remain with the class," said President Lottson. "There is a great deal of what is said here that I can't approve of, but that is all the more reason that somebody with a cool head and quick wits should be on hand to prevent the orthodox faith from going to ruin."

"I was very much interested in your remarks," said Broker Whilcher to the Judge.

" Matthew Arnold has put forth some of the same views."

" I am glad to hear it," replied the Judge. " They will save him from drifting into vacuity, and they will convince his readers of his honesty of purpose.   I wish only that I could believe that such views had as strong a hold upon the Church as they have upon the outside world. Verily, Christ never spoke a truer saying than that ' a man's foes shall be they of his own household.' "

CHAPTER VIII.

AFTERMATH.

THE closing of that session of the Scripture Club, in which the nature and reward of righteousness was discussed, did not end the consideration of the subject. Mr. Radley himself determined that, at the next meeting, some one should move the rescinding of his own resolution to allow but one Sunday to a verse of· Scripture; and several other members, among them Squire Woodhouse, Mr. Buffle, and Mr. Alleman, determined to put the resolution to death at the first opportunity. In the mean time, no member of the class, who went to and from the city on the little steamer *Oak-leaf*, nor any one who had occasion to visit the local post-office, was allowed to forget the subject, which, not for the first time, caused such widely differing theories to be offered.

"You didn't have an opportunity to express your opinions last Sunday?" said Squire Woodhouse to Mr. Alleman, at the post-office on Monday evening, while the latter awaited the opening of the mail, and the former lay in wait for some one upon whom to expend his pent-up energies.

"No," replied the teacher; "and I doubt whether the expression of them would have done any good. Men are always willing enough to be observers of a quarrel; but to take part in one generally passes for a sign of bad breeding, and the care that men have for the results of their bringing up is, under such circumstances, admirable beyond expression."

"Oh, you're not exactly fair, I think," said the Squire. "Every member of that class thinks the case of faith *vs.* works is his own; he must be interested in one side or the other, for he believes eternity depends upon it."

"I don't see why any one should have such an idea," said Mr. Alleman. "It doesn't make the slightest difference which side they take, if they really believe as they claim to do."

"Goodness!" exclaimed the Squire. "Why, are *you* going over to the defense of faith against works? You, who have always been preaching up good works as the whole end of life? I'm afraid *I've* been in too much of a hurry, for I've been drifting over to your side very, very fast during the past two or three weeks."

"I've not changed my principles in the least," replied Mr. Alleman. "Either belief includes the other, if a man is really sincere in the belief itself."

"Well," said the Squire, with humility, "you scholarly fellows can do sums in your heads at a rate that no common man's ciphering can equal. I thought I'd heard a great deal on this subject, both before I experienced a change and after, but I never could see that there could be any agreement between the two. One set of men say that faith is everything; another say that works are the thing; both sets make faces when they pass each other on Sunday on their way to their separate churches, and, if I read the religious papers correctly, it's the subject of the greatest religious fighting in the world."

"The fighting is between the men, not the ideas," said Mr. Alleman.

"Having withdrawn from the class," remarked Dr. Humbletop, who also was present, "or, I might say, having never belonged to it, I don't know that I have any right to take part in your conversation, but as this is not a stated session of the class——"

"Even if it was, Doctor, you'd be free to say whatever you liked," interrupted the Squire. "Free speech is the rule of the class on Sundays, and we certainly aren't going to be any narrower out of school than in it. Besides, you've been to a theological seminary, and know the ins and outs of this question. Now, I want to know if I'm not right and Alleman wrong?"

6*

"You certainly are correct in your assumptions," replied the reverend doctor. "The Church, or, more properly speaking, the world and the Church, have always been at war upon this important issue. It has been the cause of battles in which precious human blood was shed, as well as of struggles in which words, fiercer than spears and darts, have been the weapons used, and souls instead of bodies were to be counted among the killed and wounded."

"And the Church," remarked young Mr. Waggett, as he tore the wrapper from a religious newspaper, which the postmaster had just handed him, "our Church has decided in favor of justification by faith, as the only sure way of salvation. Other churches——"

"There are no other churches," said Dr. Humbletop. "There are societies, containing many well-meaning persons, which have works as a basis of organization. They have built edifices for worship, founded colleges and schools

for the education of youth in their ideas, established newspapers, settled persons who, by
courtesy, are called pastors, and formed societies which do much toward the amelioration of
the physical condition of unfortunate humanity.
The respect which they manifest toward portions of the Word of God renders it impossible
to deny that they possess religious feeling and
aspiration ; but to admit that they constitute a
portion of the body of which Christ is the head,
is impossible.   These persons, individually and
in their associated capacity, war against the distinctive doctrine of the Church, which is, that
Christ died for all men to make atonement for
sin, that all men may become partakers in the
benefits of this saving act by acknowledging
him to be their Lord and Saviour."

" There—I told you so," said the Squire to
the teacher.

" The Doctor has suggested a point of difference between the two great sections of the
Protestant Church," said Mr. Alleman ; " but

that was not the subject upon which we were talking."

"Why, yes, it was," said Builder Stott, who had been listening, while pretending to be otherwise engaged. "I heard every word of it."

Mr. Alleman gave an impatient start. "I said the disagreement was between men, and not between ideas. Our good champion of orthodoxy, the Doctor, cannot, with due respect to his Maker, admit that there are any works of real value that are not prompted by a true belief in the principles enounced by Jesus. Faith implies trust; trust of the inferior in the superior signifies a willingness to be guided: the guidance of a Being in whose wisdom and love we have unlimited confidence *must* be followed, if we really believe His utterances, and believe our own nature to be as imperfect and sinful as we profess to think it is."

"Ah!" said Dr. Humbletop, "theories of human action may be very beautiful, but that very imperfection and sinfulness of man makes them of no effect. Logically, Mr. Alleman is perfectly correct, and, from his very assertions, the Church deduces the argument whereby she brings reason to the support of inspiration. Man is so imperfect, so sinful, so depraved, that, when he would do good, evil is ever present with him. This condition of man shows the absolute need of a Saviour, and, of course, a loving God will not allow his children to lack anything which they really need. Thus the need and the existence of a Saviour are established, by their interdependence upon each other."

"That is hardly the point of our conversation," said Mr. Alleman. "The question between us was, whether there was not a similar interdependence between faith and works; whether, as either of them logically implies the other, either is not logically inclusive of the other."

"Works include faith?" exclaimed Builder Stott. "Well, excuse me, but my time is valuable, and I guess I'll be moving. I always like to get hold of a real idea about religion, but that notion is too far-fetched for anything. Why, according to you, a Unitarian or a heathen, if he does good, is a child of God and a partaker of the promises. Christ might as well not have lived and died, if that is all his work amounted to."

Mr. Stott started, and Squire Woodhouse exclaimed, " Why don't you keep him?"

" Because," said Mr. Alleman, with a peculiar smile, " I'm occasionally orthodox enough to believe that some men are predestinated to destruction, and that men, like Stott, who never follow Christ's teachings and dread them as they do Satan, are among the number. Honestly, now, Squire Woodhouse, can you see how a sincere attempt to fulfill the moral injunctions of Jesus Christ and his apostles can fail to lead a man to faith in Christ and the Father? When a system of morality is given, which, in terms and results, is so far above the morality of the world that the world shrinks

from it, yet which in practice proves to be correct, do you suppose it is possible to doubt the
higher inspiration of the giver? Did any mere
law-giver ever enjoin unselfishness? Is unselfishness natural? Does not its practice, and the
spiritual influence which is felt in return for its
practice, raise a man to a plane of wisdom, ten-
derness, and strength, such as has never been
reached in any other way? Have not honest
disbelievers in great numbers, when they have
attempted a higher morality than that of the
world in general, fallen back upon Christ as
their only available teacher, and been led to
him, either by desperation or sympathy, or
both ? "

The Squire had not read as much as Mr. Alleman in the controversial theological literature
of the day, and he could not reply from actual
knowledge, but he said :

" I don't know, but I'll take your word for it.
I know that although I'm a church member, and
pretend to be led by the Spirit, there have been

only once in a while times when I've got outside of business rules about matters of time and
money, and that, when these times have come,
I've felt nearer to God than I've ever done
even when I've been in trouble."

"Then you understand my meaning," said
Mr. Alleman. "There is no difference between
faith and works, providing both are rendered in
sincerity, for neither of them can help leading to
the other. And as you have seen the truth of
this fact by personal experience, you are just
the man who should support me in the effort
which I hope to make next Sunday to impress
this truth upon the class, not for the sake of pre-
senting a new theory for discussion, but to join
conflicting ideas for the good of man and the
glory of God."

"I frankly admit," said Dr. Humbletop,
"that friend Alleman's idea is a beautiful one—
so beautiful that it could not have been conceived without inspiration from on high. But
should it prevail in society instead of being con-

fined to the individual breast, its results can hardly fail to be disastrous. What will restrain depraved humanity from neglecting the offer of salvation by faith in Christ, and devote itself to working out its own salvation? How many souls will be lost if the fear of eternal suffering is not held before them, and if they attempt to begin through work, and finish ere the blessed time of change comes?"

"If they can trust to God's mercy while they are mere beggars for help," said Mr. Alleman, "they can certainly do it while they are endeavoring to help themselves and Him. Unless," continued Mr. Alleman, with an impatient gesture, "unless God can seem to you to be nothing but a vengeful monster—unless he has at some unknown time withdrawn all his merciful promises to those who do righteousness and walk uprightly."

"My dear young friend," said Dr. Humbletop, who had slowly been dropping his head backward and adding intensity to the solicitude ex-

pressed by his stare, "do you know that you
have taken upon yourself the authority to urge
men from the new dispensation back to the
old, and thus to set back the work of grace for
two thousand years? Do you not know that
the law alone was found to be insufficient?"

"Do *you* not know," said Mr. Alleman, "that
by that assertion you impugn the wisdom of the
Almighty?"

"God forbid!" exclaimed the doctor, starting backward so abruptly that he nearly over-
turned the post-office stove. "The law was
given as it was on account of the hardness
of men's hearts, as Christ himself expressly
states."

"True," said Mr. Alleman, "and 'the times
of this ignorance God winked at, but now com-
mandeth all men to repent.' When the law was
insufficient to the needs of mankind, God sent
another law-giver in the person of Christ. And
men might have obeyed him to a greater extent
than they do, had not the Church taken the po-

sition that the need of man was of more consequence than duty to God, and that saving
one's self—which human selfishness is abund-
antly able to look out for without being urged
to it—is of more consequence than comply-
ing with the desires of Christ, and through
Christ, God."

"Salvation possible through human selfishness!" ejaculated Dr. Humbletop.

"That's the sentiment which the church most
appeals to," said Mr. Alleman.

"The central truth of inspiration, revelation,
and the atonement only a concession to the fears
and personal desires of mankind!" continued
the doctor. "Oh, horrible, horrible!"

"It *is* horrible," said Mr. Alleman, "that a
strong organization like the Church, with re-
spectability, morality, tradition, and authority on
its side, should teach such a doctrine; but your
own sermons, which I have found to be models
of logic, though based upon false premises,
prove the truth of your condensation of my

statements. Men are urged, not to righteousness as taught by prophets, apostles, and the
Master himself, but to take the best possible
care of Number One—urged to something
which the most miserable savage alive knows
is dictated by the strongest instinct of his nature.
What must Christ, remembering the intensity
and agony of his earthly efforts, think of the
Church ?"

Dr. Humbletop assumed, slowly, his pulpit
manner, and at length replied :

"My dear friend—for dear I must call you
in remembrance of your many self-denying
efforts for the good of mankind—I must decline
to discuss this subject any further with you.
For two thousand years the Church of Christ
has endured, and guided itself according to the
words of Christ himself—"

"All of his words, or only such of them as
have been fullest of promise of safety ?" interrupted Mr. Alleman.

"All of them," boldly replied the doctor.

"The Church has taught everything that Christ did. I, myself, have preached from every verse of Christ's sermon on the Mount."

"But you have carefully avoided the literal meanings of these verses in nearly every instance," said Mr. Alleman.

"I have attached to each one such meaning as the Spirit has indicated to me," said the doctor, with rather chilling dignity. "And I would further say that I have treated them according to the habit of the Church during the nineteen centuries that have nearly elapsed since Christ appeared. If I had taught from my own understanding alone, I might have had misgivings; but with countless prophets, apostles, and martyrs to whom to look for example, I have felt secure in my position. You cannot, therefore, expect me to accept your views as opposed to those of the whole body of Christian teachers. The experience of the world is always of value in teaching the teacher what to do and say, and that experience—"

"Is always based upon selfishness," interrupted Mr. Alleman.

"And that experience," continued Dr. Humbletop, "has been that the atonement made by Christ is the all in all of Scripture."

The doctor called for his letters, bowed in a dignified manner to Mr. Alleman and the Squire, and departed.

Let no one blame Dr. Humbletop for his lack of clear vision. A more honest, conscientious, and generous soul could not be found in Valley Rest. Receiving an income which to many of his acquaintances would have seemed insufficient to a man of good breeding and refined tastes, he found ways of devoting more than a tithe of it to charities either private or public. He was always ready to forego his own tastes and inclinations in order to visit the sick, counsel the troubled, or pray with the dying; his voice and vote were never lacking in affairs of public interest, and they were always used in the interest of the highest morality. But the

doctor had been born and bred under a religious system which he had been taught was to
be accepted, not changed, and not even to be
questioned. To him, as to the wise Solomon,
the law of the Lord was perfect, the difference
between the two men being that the doctor found
the whole law in the letter of a single depart-
ment of it, instead of in the Spirit, and that
this peculiarity of his mind had come to him
by birth, been strengthened by a special education, and established by habit. Whenever he
for a moment questioned his belief, he very
naturally contemplated the many generations
of wiser men who had accepted beliefs like his
own, and in their wisdom and their interpretation of Scripture his soul rested.

And yet Squire Woodhouse was moved to
say to Mr. Alleman :

" It seems to me the doctor begs the question."

CHAPTER IX.

THE DOCTRINE OF INSURANCE.

CONVERSATION upon the lesson of the previous Sunday was not confined to the quartette that met at the village post-office. Most of the members of the club went to the city on Monday morning on the little steamer *Oak-leaf.* The radicals among them were eager for a renewal of the fray, and the orthodox were not at all averse to displaying their defensive abilities. Indeed, President Lottson stood at the wharf, newspaper in hand, for the express purpose of encountering Broker Whilcher, and provoking him to make an attack. The broker finally appeared, accompanied by his wife and children ; but the presence of non-combatants did not discourage the Soldier of the Cross, who had been too long in the insurance business to be willing to lose any chance of strengthening his own protection against risk in another world. Broker Whilcher met him boldly ; he sent his *impedimenta* promptly to the rear—to wit, the ladies' saloon—and prepared for the combat which he knew was approaching.

"I suppose you think you whipped us yesterday," said President Lottson, by way of opening shot.

"It was too clear a case to depend upon supposition only," said the broker ; "but if you've any doubts on the subject I've no objections to helping defeat you again."

"Seriously, Whilcher," said the president, leading his antagonist to a *tête-à-tête*, "do you realize what comes of all this nonsense ? You profess to be a free-thinker, so I won't ask you to meet me on my own ground, which is that the new dispensation furnishes a substitute for the old ; I'll only ask you to look at the matter from your own rationalistic point of view. A man must live up to his beliefs, if he *is* a man."

7

"True enough," replied the broker. "I wish your parson would admit the same, and preach accordingly. I wouldn't be cheated quite so often by his parishioners."

"Business is business," said the president. "You don't ever let any of the theories of your new-fashioned philosophy stand in the way of your making a good trade, do you?"

"No, I can't say that I do," replied the broker.

"And yet," said Mr. Lottson, "you believe in the theory of the reign of law—a law which cannot be broken without danger of severe penalty. Now whether Christ was God or only man, you've got to obey the law under penalty of punishment, unless there is some other way of satisfying it. Therefore, why not accept a belief that leaves you as free to believe in the law, to admire its wisdom and beauty, as you are now? Putting the thing in a business light, you change no beliefs—you simply take on a new one."

"I'll profess to believe nothing but what I understand," declared the broker.

"You believe in geography, don't you?" asked the president, "and in history, astronomy, chemistry, zoölogy—all the sciences, in fact? You swear by Darwin, yet you certainly don't pretend to understand all that he writes about."

"I accept his conclusions, because I believe in his wisdom and honesty," said the broker. "Of course I don't profess to be able to follow him through his scientific experiments."

"Exactly," said the president. "And you believe that Christ and the apostles were honest, don't you?"

"Yes—as honest as *human* beings ever are," said the broker.

"That means as honest as Darwin and Spencer, then," said Mr. Lottson. "Then why not believe them as well as your scientific teachers?"

"Because——" said Mr. Whilcher, and hesitated.

" Because other people *do*," continued Lott-son, " and it wouldn't seem scholarly to accept that which was taught and accepted by men whose demonstrations were not made by the as-sistance of material things. If you stick to your ideas, men will hold you to them. You can't live up to them in your business ; you'll lose money if you try it, and you'll be called a fool for your pains. Why don't you be consistent ? There's no consistency between morals and business excepting through the medium of the Christian belief. Believe what you choose so long as you believe in a First Cause, be one of us, accept the promises that were made to pro-vide for your condition as well as that of every other man that finds a constant disagreement between life and law. Then you'll at least have done what is the business duty of every man— you'll have provided against the dangers which you don't fear, and yet daren't defy for fear they may exist."

" That's a cold-blooded way of putting it, any

way," remarked the broker, after a moment or two of thought, which was apparently amusing.

"I don't deny it," said the president, "but reason is always cold-blooded. You don't pretend that in your darling scientific hobbies it's anything else, do you? You free-thinkers claim to monopolize reason ; but you can't help seeing that religion deals in it just as much as science does, and that it leads men to the church as truly as it does to the study. And I want it ·to lead you to us, as it is bound to do if you're as fair as you pretend to be."

"You want me to be a religionist, do you ?" asked Whilcher ; "a shouting, sentimental exhorter! What a fine reputation you want me to make—and lose—among my friends !"

"I don't want you to do anything of the sort," said the president. "Did you ever hear of *me* shouting or exhorting ?"

Mr. Whilcher laughed long and loud at the mere thought, as would any other of the president's acquaintances have done. The president

colored a little and contemplated the matting of
the cabin floor, but replied :

" It's nothing to my discredit, nor anything to
laugh about.   Because excitable people get into
the church, drawn there by appeals to their
emotional nature, it doesn't prove that noise
and talk are necessary results of religion.   You
don't find any nonsense of that kind in St. Paul's
Epistles, do you ?   *He* was a man after my own
heart—a fellow who believed that the laborer
was worthy of his hire, who kept himself before
the people, who talked solid sense, and explained how easy it was for every man to take
advantage of the sacrifice that was made for
him.   You know the little company there is in
the city that insures against accidents?   I don't
believe you'd lend twenty-five cents on the dollar on its stock—I'll sell you some of their cer-
tificates cheaper than that, if you ever want any
—but whenever you make a trip out of town I
understand you take out one of their policies."

" So I do," said the broker.   " It costs very

little, and it covers a good deal, and may come handy in case of trouble."

"That's exactly the argument in favor of your joining the church," said the president, "excepting that in the latter case a great deal more is promised and the cost is nothing at all."

"Excepting church dues," said the broker, with a quizzical smile.

"Well," said the president, "that's true, but what do they amount to in a question of risk?"

Broker Whilcher reflected profoundly for several moments, and at last said:

"Lottson, I'm inclined to do it; if any one had ever talked solid sense to me about religion I should have been in the Church before. Still, how am I going to solemnly declare before a body of people that I believe things which I really don't believe at all?"

"You must believe them before you declare any belief, and believe them for the reason that you believe thousands of other things—because you are told that they are true. You believe many a thing on the word of worse men than those who wrote the Gospels and Epistles, for these men showed no sign of being on the make, while your business informants do. You are to believe them for lack of any definite information to the contrary, and because there was no selfish object in the eye of any man who gave the words upon which these beliefs are founded."

"I declare, I'll do it!" exclaimed the broker; "but say, Lottson, do you get a commission on church members as you do on insurance risks? Because if you do—halves!"

"Nonsense!" laughed the president. "You'll have to go before the examining committee this week, for next Sunday is the first of the month, and the regular day for the reception of new members."

"Examining committee!" exclaimed the broker. "Whew! I guess I'll change my mind."

"Don't be afraid," said the president. "I'm a member of the committee, myself, and when

I take a candidate in hand, the others are pretty sure to let him alone. I've been in business long enough to know how to treat a man according to his style, I fancy."

The new candidate laughed heartily to himself, stared at the president so intently that he embarrassed the latter ; then he shook his head with the air of a man to whom a new revelation had come, and he put a cigar in his mouth and started forward for a contemplative smoke.

As for President Lottson, he quoted to himself, with intense satisfaction, the passage :

" Whoso shall convert a sinner from the error of his ways shall save a soul from death and cover a multitude of sins."

Then he searched the boat diligently for Captain Maile, and when he had found him he told him the news with evident exultation, and the captain replied :

" Another crooked stick reserved unto the final burning."

" See here, Maile," said Mr. Lottson, " this is

7*

nonsense, and you're the last man who should be guilty of it. Your father and grandfather were among the founders of the church in this section of country."

"That's true," said the captain, "and to save the family reputation from disgrace, I've had to spend some of the money they left me in trying to undo some of the mischief they did."

"Then you're a fool," said the president. "That may sound like plain talk, but it's true; you should have learned, as your ancestors did, that religion is one thing and business is another."

"Oh, I've learned it," said the captain, "and I've also learned that the devil, if there is a devil, is the father of that precious notion, and that it's worth millions to him. Do you suppose I think any more of men because they belong to the church? Do you imagine I look over your policies any less carefully than I do those of Bennett, who don't believe in God, devil, or anybody else? Do you suppose I'll take Whilcher's word a minute quicker when he gets into the church than I do now? Not a bit of it. The church is the hope of the honest and the mask of the rascally. How did you like the way the lesson went yesterday?"

"I liked the way it ended better than anything else," said the president.

"I knew you would," said the captain; "and if they spring a reconsideration on you next Sunday, *won't* you be disgusted!"

Mr. Buffle had approached the couple as they conversed, and said:

"Gentlemen, what do you think of yesterday's exercises?"

"Both dissatisfied," promptly replied the captain. "Lottson don't like the way they began, and I'm sorry that they ended when they did."

"I'm counting noses to see if we can't secure a reconsideration," said Mr. Buffle. "I don't like the way in which the main question was dodged, and I want to hear more of it."

"Then you'd better go over to the Unitarian

Church," said President Lottson. "They'll talk morality to you there to your heart's content."

"They will in our church, too," replied Mr. Buffle, "unless prevented by trickery. One would suppose that morality was something to be afraid of by the way people dodge talking about it."

Mr. Lottson assumed a very high-toned air, and replied :

" It isn't that morality is feared, but that when men fall to talking about it they forget that there is anything higher."

" Perhaps it's because they never talk about it excepting at the beginning," said Mr. Buffle, " and they're anxious to begin at the bottom, as men have to do in business and everything else, if they really want to learn. I begin to think it's a subject about which there isn't much known. It's often seemed to me in churches that men are very much like the apprentices in my ship-yard; the first thing these boys want to do is to paint the names and designs on the paddle-boxes, though that's the very last thing we generally attend to. Not one in a hundred of them are ever anxious to know how keels are laid and hulls are shaped."

"That's only business; isn't it, Lottson?" asked Captain Maile. "Business and religion are two very different things, and a smart man like you, Buffle, ought to know it, and not go about arranging for Sunday exercises to torment men into thinking what they ought to do, instead of letting them enjoy a day of holy rest and delight in the contemplation of what they're going to get when they can't stay here any longer to get for themselves."

Mr. Lottson turned abruptly away, and remarked to Mr. Prymm that Captain Maile was the most hardened scoffer he had ever known. He also informed Prymm of the movement in favor of a reconsideration of the lesson of the previous Sunday.

"I shall oppose it," said Mr. Prymm with more than his ordinary decision. "I entered the class with the hope of learning something of God's will as revealed by the Scriptures; but if it is the desire of the remaining members, or a majority of them, that we shall linger for weeks over single verses, I shall find it more convenient and profitable to devote the corresponding hour of every Sabbath to private study and contemplation."

"I suppose," said President Lottson, noting the approach of Judge Cottaway and Deacon Bates elbow to elbow, the latter looking very solemn and the judge exceedingly bored, "I suppose it will be like Cottaway to insinuate that the matter should be talked over and over again until doomsday. It takes a lawyer to string a subject out until he doesn't know the end of it when he sees it."

"Lawyers like the judge have some faculties which we might imitate with profit," said Mr. Buffle. "They believe in listening to all the evidence and determining accordingly. Evidence seems a something which the members of this class are afraid of, and practice based upon it is still more terrifying. Ah, good morning, judge—we want to have another talk next Sunday on the subject of yesterday's lesson, and knowing your experience in sifting evidence, we would be very grateful if you would charge your conscience with the case, and become responsible for it."

"If the rule can be suspended, I shall be glad to throw upon it such light as I can," said the judge.

"We were talking, gentlemen," said Deacon Bates, "upon the spiritual significance of righteousness. I suggested, and the judge was pleased to agree with me, that righteousness had a spiritual as well as a merely moral significance."

"It certainly has," said President Lottson promptly, "and if for a while we could divest ourselves of the materialistic notions which prevail as badly in the Church as out of it, we would obtain some new light on this subject which is so puzzling when considered only by the human mind. We would realize that with the prince of this world Christ has nothing to do ; that while in the world we are under the dominion of the world."

"And that our real life does not begin until we are with God," said Deacon Bates, by way of supplement. "This world is a place of preparation for another, and it is what we are to do and be in that blessed sphere that Christ came to teach us. The things of this world are really the unreal—only the things which are unseen are eternal. How much righteousness had the crucified thief who rebuked his fellow for reviling Christ? Yet to him were spoken the words which every Christian longs to hear, 'This day shalt thou be with me in Paradise.' Belief in Christ, longing for him and his glory, are what should occupy our thoughts while on earth."

"And do it so closely that we shall have an opportunity to follow him. Of course when a man believes in a presidential candidate, he believes and does nothing else.   He doesn't vote for him, act according to his political theories, spend money for him, or any such nonsense. He merely believes in him, and does or leaves undone everything else, feeling sure that it's the candidate's business to make everything come right.   That isn't the way you gentlemen talked last campaign, though."

The deacon smiled pityingly.   "There you go again," said he, "mixing the temporal and the spiritual, though they're not the slightest bit alike."

"Certainly not," said Captain Maile ; "so it's heretical to try to bring heavenly influences to bear upon earthly things.   You want people to understand that God is not God of the living, but of the dead, though that wasn't the way Christ said it when he was alive."

Each man put on a pugnacious face, and betook himself to his own reflections, and these lasted until the boat touched her pier in the city.

CHAPTER X.

A DECISIVE BATTLE.

WHEN the Scripture Club assembled on the following Sunday, it was in a manner somewhat more quiet and less cordial than usual. Mr. Jodderel volunteered the opening prayer, and then Deacon Bates began to read the fifth beatitude, when Mr. Radley said :

"Mr. Leader, a majority of the class would like to hear a further discussion of the last subject. As the original mover of the resolution restricting the class to one Sunday to a verse, which motion I made with the almost unanimous support of the class, it is fitting that I should take the initiative in securing a further hearing upon any subject of which the majority have not heard enough. I therefore move that

162

the rule referred to be rescinded for one Sunday, and that we continue the discussion of the fourth beatitude."

"Second the motion," said Squire Woodhouse.

"Mr. Leader," exclaimed Mr. Jodderel, "I object. The time of this class should be spent upon the consideration of subjects according to their relative importance. If the nature and whereabouts of the Kingdom of Heaven is worth only a single hour of discussion, this minor question of righteousness certainly isn't entitled to any more. I must oppose the resolution."

"It was apparently very unwise to adopt such a rule," remarked Mr. Prymm, "if only to be rescinded or suspended whenever the curiosity of any of the members may desire it. We are adults instead of children, and cannot afford, for the sake of consistency, the abrogation of this rule, especially when every one present has unlimited informal and social opportunities for discussion, as, indeed, they have already been doing all week long."

Mr. Prymm looked appealingly toward President Lottson, but that gentleman seemed in the depths of a gloomy reverie, and unwilling to be disturbed. For Mr. Lottson's convert had relapsed; he had, before the evening on which the examining committee met, dropped a note to Mr. Lottson, saying that the longer he meditated upon the matter the more he felt that the proposed action would be hypocritical; that if the church would not detect the hypocrisy, the rest of the world would, and he preferred to retain the respect of his friends. This note of Broker Whilcher's had not only inflicted disappointment upon President Lottson, but it had brought him some tormenting anxieties. If Whilcher, who was a shrewd observer of men, really meant what he said, was it not possible and probable that he, President Lottson, who believed all that he had asked the broker to believe, and very little more, might also be looked upon as a hypocrite? He knew that his reputation in his own church was not all that he could have wished it to be; but, looked at in sober earnest, his church, to his eyes, consisted of such of its members as were city business men, like himself; there was still another element in the church, however, and it was numerically the largest, which judged a man by his professions, and Mr. Lottson trusted that among these he still retained his respect. But then came a more annoying thought. Business was business, and business men would take no man's word any the more implicitly because he was a church member. Could it be possible that among these he passed not only for a business man of ordinary morality, but as a hypocrite too? Was he not really honest in his beliefs? He certainly was; he could lay his hand on his heart and swear honestly that every religious belief he possessed he had acquired by the exercise of his best logical faculties. Why, then, should he be considered hypocritical? Could it be possible that the world saw something more in the Bible than church members like himself did? Certainly not. How could the world do anything of the sort? It had never studied the Bible as he had done, and as fathers of the faith, with whom he had never for a moment dared to compare himself, had done. And then to have a prolonged consideration of the late lesson go on in his hearing while he felt as he did! It was unendurable. He would have departed silently and without explanation, and betaken himself to Dr. Humbletop's class, had he not previously informed Builder Stott that he would remain and look after orthodox interests in the club.

But as he reached this point of his reflections, Mr. Prymm's remarks ended, and his eye caught Mr. Prymm's, and the exasperating character of the doctrine of non-paying works seemed more unendurable to him than ever, so he controlled himself, rose to his feet, and said:

"Mr. Leader, in the interest of Christianity,

as defined by the Master, I also object to the
further consideration of this subject, if it is urged
with the spirit that has been manifested. Christ
said, 'My yoke is easy and my burden is light,'
but some of the members of this class remind
me of the Pharisees of whom Christ said that
'they bound upon men's shoulders burdens
grievous to be borne.' If religion was made
for anything, it was made for belief and use in
this present world ; I object, therefore, to its
being made to appear so unlovely and severe
that those who most need it are frightened from
it.   Those of us who believe would never have
done so had we supposed that men would be
allowed to set aside Christ's merciful words, and
establish the commandments—the notions—of
men in their place.   I believe as thoroughly in
righteousness as any man, but I don't care to
sit here and listen to its meaning being changed
by men who care more for their own opinions
than they do for the commandments of God.
And so I shall vote against the resolution, and

ask all others to do so, if they believe in the righteousness of God instead of that of man."

" I don't see why it's a Scriptural subject at all," said Mr. Hopper, relinquishing for a moment his hold upon the review containing the article on " The True Location of the Holy Sepulchre." " It was announced by Jesus, I know ; but it was before he made that atonement which set aside mere human righteousness as a requisite to salvation. I move we drop the subject."

" The gentleman's motion is not in order, unless in the form of an amendment," said Deacon Bates.

" Mr. Hopper's suggestion that this beatitude was given before the atonement was made," said young Mr. Waggett, "is so original and so full of practical interest that I should like to hear a further discussion of the subject, if only to see whether this point cannot be substantiated—or, rather, whether it can be successfully opposed."

President Lottson leaned over the back of young Mr. Waggett's chair, and whispered:

"Don't make an ass of yourself. *I* can see where this thing is bound to lead us, if you can't; vote the other way when the question is put."

A moment or two of silence ensued, and then Deacon Bates put the question to vote. A strong response of "Ay!" was soon followed by an equally noisy "No!" and some one called for a rising vote. Up rose Judge Cottaway, Squire Woodhouse, Broker Whilcher, Mr. Radley, Principal Alleman, Mr. Buffle, Lawyer Scott, Dr. Fahrenglotz, and Captain Maile, nine in all, while for the negative there were but seven votes, Mr. Bungfloat and young Banty keeping their seats during both votes, the former with a helpless expression of countenance, and the latter with a contemptuous smile.

"The ayes have it," said the leader, and Builder Stott, who, until that moment, had listened at the key-hole, hurried off to Dr. Humbletop's class-room and stated that the club was determined on carrying free speech into the ground and the club with it.

"Mark my words," said the builder, "the Scripture Club is as good as dead."

The discussion was opened by Judge Cottaway, according to the special request of the founder of the club, and the old jurist spoke as follows:

"Estimated according to the rules of evidence, the requirement for righteousness never ends in the Holy Scriptures, and never can end while the Church hold the revealed will of God as an authoritative rule of guidance. The law was the topic of lawgivers, prophets, the Psalmist, the wise Solomon, and all of them regarded it as the only substitute for the personal presence and command of God. Christ never failed to hold it up for reverence and obedience, excepting when minor points of it were of less vital importance than that of those for whose direction it was given."

"That's it, exactly," interrupted Mr. Jod-

derel. "The law was made for man, not man
for the law, and when man can't live according
to the law, the law must give way, as it did
by express command when Christ condemned
the Jews for rebuking the disciples when they
plucked corn on the Sabbath day."

"I imagine that it was more for the sake of
rebuking hypocrisy than to defend the improvi-
dence of his disciples that Christ spoke as he
did on the occasion referred to," said the judge.
"But he declared the binding force of the law
more than once, and he not only urged it upon
the people, but increased its scope and severity
by explaining that obedience should not be
only to the letter, but to the spirit of the heavenly commands. Mercy, love, and compassion
are not at all inconsistent with the closest application of the law, though men have strangely
come to imagine that they are. In this same
matchless sermon we are studying you will find
his definition of some methods of violating the
seventh commandment. The spiritual rule

from which Christ deduced these conclusions
may be applied to all the other commandments
with results equally startling. ' Thou shalt not
steal,' is the simple letter of the eighth commandment, but according to the new method
prescribed by Christ for the translation of the
law according to Moses, to deprive a man of
his peace, of his patience, of his faith in mankind, even if done in ways permissible in business circles, is as truly theft as is the depriving
a man of his money by actual robbery. And
as I am a member of the bar, as I have been a
law-maker, and an adjudicator of legal questions, I feel that I am severe upon no one more
than my own old self, when I say that to recover the amount of a debt by legal means
which compel the debtor to part with property
of value several times greater than that of the
property upon which the debt is based, is theft
of the most heinous description, for even under
the most merciful construction of the most
careless law, the only theft at all pardonable is

that of small amounts in cases of dire necessity; whereas my experience in legal collections is that not once in a hundred times are they made excepting of men in the direst distress, and of utter inability to pay."

"But Christ mercifully forbore to give such interpretations to all the commandments," said Mr. Jodderel, "and I have always thought his refraining from doing so was one of the sure proofs of his divinity. Of course he saw the people around him—his own disciples, even—doing hundreds of things that were wrong; but he knew their natures were too feeble to live up to the holy ideas which were natural enough to *Him*, so he said little, except to exhort them to sin no more."

"Very true," said the judge, "but since then the Christian world has had the benefit of nearly twenty centuries of growth under the instructions of Christ. Men have grown less animal, more intellectual; less brutal, more spiritual. The passions and appetites that once seemed uncontrollable have come more and more under restraint under the influence of generations of right living. Men nowadays endure physical discipline from which the ascetics of Christ's time, or even of the middle ages, would have shrunk with fear. The world is lamentably full of wickedness and weakness, but it has now what it did *not* have when Moses gave his law—it has in every community one or more men who show by right living what a perfect control man may exert over his lower faculties, or, rather, over the lower developments of faculties which in the clearer light of to-day develop into noble virtues. But the stronger sins die hardest, so to-day we find, in communities where murder is unheard of, Sabbath-breaking unknown, profanity unspoken, and the greater crimes mentioned in the Decalogue seldom or never brought to light—in such localities we find the greed of gain made the excuse of unfair dealings between man and man ; it stirs up strife more vicious than that which took place when the civilized world was one grand camp, and when to kill a man for his possessions was a deed praiseworthy rather than otherwise, especially when the victim might, with any excuse, be called an enemy."

"One might suppose, from the judge's remarks, that the world had but one sin—and only one virtue," said Mr. Jodderel.

"According to Scripture," exclaimed the judge, "there *is* but one virtue, for it includes all others. Its name is Love—will the gentleman remember that the assertion is Christ's, and not mine? There is more than one sin, truly ; but not one of the dreadful number could exist were the one virtue practiced as it should be. And this brings me back to the leading idea of the lesson, from which I have unintentionally been diverted toward specialties. And yet, I know not how better to explain the nature of righteousness according to the law, than to continue in use the illustration that I have been using—the treatment, by each other, of men in their business affairs. For there are but few relations of men that cannot be classified under business heads. By implication, sins against self and nature belong in the same category, for the man who impairs in any way his own physical and mental capital, injures to a greater or less extent the whole community in which he resides. To save man and to bless him is the whole aim of the law, for it is only by man in his proper condition that God can be fully glorified. Thus regarded, the way of righteousness can never seem hard, tiresome, or narrow—it is rather the only highway which is always delightful. The promise given, therefore, in this beatitude is the most precious in the whole Bible, for there is no good it does not include, nor any evil which it does not help us to shun."

"That's the first satisfactory description I ever heard of the law," remarked Mr. Radley. "I wonder why other men—preachers, even—never talk about it in the same way."

"They'd lose all their wealthy pew-holders if they did," answered Captain Maile.

"Not all," said Mr. Buffle, "at least, not if *I'm* as well off in this world's goods as I think I am. And I don't propose to forget what I have heard."

"It is very evident, however," said President Lottson, "that Christ knew that this idea of the law—which I admit to be as sound as it is beautiful—could never be fulfilled by man, or he would never have considered it necessary to make an atonement for sin, and urge people to accept it, instead of trying to be saved by righteousness alone. The gentleman lays great stress upon the failings of business men. They exist about as he has painted them, but had he spent his own life in business instead of among the abstractions of a learned profession, he would see the other side of the case, which is that business is selfish, that it cannot be otherwise, and that man's only hope lies in Christ's promises."

8*

"Only hope of what?" asked Squire Wood-house.

"Of salvation, of course," replied the president.

"Then, what about the world?" asked Mr. Radley. "Is nothing to be done *here* for God —and man? Did we come into the world for no purpose but to get out of it in the best shape we can? Has God no purposes to fulfill here, or did he only make this wonderful combination of beauty and utility, that we call the world, to be a mere stage for blundering and wrong-doing?"

"No," answered young Mr. Waggett; "it is to fit us all for entrance to the glorious company of angels, prophets, and martyrs."

"We had better all die in infancy then," said Mr. Radley, "before we've been unfitted for such society, and been compelled to begin all over again. What a contemptible blunderer God must be, if the common religious idea of the use of the world is correct!"

"Gentlemen," said Mr. Alleman, "it seems to me that this class has by this time plainly indicated its religious measure. We have met together many times; we have expressed our own views, and listened to many others; we have individually indicated considerable ability and ingenuity; but I am unable to discover that even a respectable minority have changed their beliefs. Of the sincerity of belief of those who have spoken there can be no doubt; but something more than ability and sincerity is necessary to retain usefulness for a body of men, who are determined to approach intellectually no nearer to each other. As we cannot agree intellectually, why can we not do so morally, and establish for the class a higher motive than can be furnished by religious curiosity or tenacity of special theological opinions? Free speech has been the distinctive feature of the class, but all that freedom of expression can gain for us has already been gained. Why cannot we, therefore, form a new and solemn compact that we will, each one according to his own special religious belief and light, strictly order our lives according to the moral ideas which we all admit are found in the Bible and are above criticism?"

"What!" exclaimed Mr. Jodderel, "and turn a religious organization into a society for the encouragement of mere morality? None for me!"

"I should consider such a course as religiously suicidal, if not blasphemous," declared Mr. Prymm.

"The man who does it can bid good-bye to his property," said Mr. Hopper, "and I, for one, am determined to give a good account of my stewardship."

"He can bid good-bye to his chance of salvation, too," said young Mr. Waggett, "if he's not going to think more of it than he does of mere morality."

"Good-bye to his fun, too," suggested young Mr. Banty.

"If we cannot leave all to follow Him," re-marked Deacon Bates, who had once felt himself called to mission work, but successfully resisted the call, "it would certainly be unseemly to do so for the sake of mere worldly righteousness."

"'Twould revolutionize society," said Law-yer Scott, "and no man should attempt such a thing without the most careful preparation."

"Doesn't Herbert Spencer say something about morality being at the top of everything?" asked Mr. Buffle of Broker Whilcher.

"Ye—es," said the broker; "but he consid-ers that it's wrong to sacrifice one's business, as I'd have to do to live according to the plan suggested."

"If Christ had intended that morality should have been so much," said President Lottson, "he would have talked more about it, and less about other things. He knew what the world needed, what it could stand, and what it couldn't."

"As if he wasn't all the while insisting upon

morality," exclaimed Mr. Alleman. " Captain
Maile, you're certainly with us! You've always talked as if you were."

The captain made a wry face.

" I've talked against hypocrisy—that's what
I've done," said he. " I've got no special religious belief myself, but I hate to see holes in
those of other people."

" I," said Dr. Fahrenglotz, " would yield ad-
herence to such a system, were it not that men
disagree as to what morality is, and I do not
wish to subject myself to any arbitrary rule or
agreement. The soul of man should be free."

Judge Cottaway arose and gave his hand to
Mr. Alleman, and several members affected to
consider this action as a sign that the meeting
had adjourned. The party dispersed more rapidly than it had ever done before, and left the
judge, the principal, the Squire, Mr. Buffle, and
Mr. Radley talking to each other.

CHAPTER XI.

CONCLUSION.

WHEN next the Scripture Club convened
there were visible some vacant places.
Mr. Alleman was not there, and Mr. Prymm
had betaken himself to Dr. Humbletop's class,
where he might study the Word of God without
perplexing annoyances from those who could
not, for even an hour in a week, and that hour
on the Sabbath day, let the world out of their
thoughts. Several of the members had endeavored to dissuade Mr. Prymm from his intention, but he remained firm. Broker Whilcher
went back to his Unitarian brethren, but even
among them he was noted as having lost his old
interest in the brotherhood of man and the
rights of humanity. Young Mr. Banty drifted
off to nowhere in particular ; but for weeks he

told to every irreligious acquaintance the story of the difficulties in the Scripture Club, and great was the sinful hilarity excited thereby.

The difference of opinion on the subject of righteousness had upon the class an effect so peculiar that Dr. Fahrenglotz did not hesitate to express an opinion that free speech was a dead letter, and he thereafter took pains to absent himself from the company of the assumed custodians thereof, although he was frequently and earnestly besought to favor the club with the pure logical aspect of questions, the import of which the members had first obscured by much sophistry.

Judge Cottaway, Squire Woodhouse, Principal Alleman, Mr. Radley, and the founder of the class contracted a habit of meeting informally at each other's residence, and as subscription papers increased in numbers soon after, there was little or no curiosity manifested by their late associates to know what was talked about at these meetings. It was a noteworthy fact, and the subject of much dismal head-shaking among the churchly, that these five men represented four different denominations, and that they finally deprived Father McGarry's flock of a member who had several times listened to the discussions of the club in its earlier days, whom they failed to provide with a new denominational faith in place of his old one.

As for Captain Maile, he was thereafter the most shamefaced and silent man at Valley Rest. He was by no means the first man who had mistaken the critical faculty for character; but he was not a man of large information in the history of the world outside of Valley Rest, so he spent several years of his life in indignant yet humble self-questionings as to his peculiar mental organization. He finally admitted to himself that to keep his fault-finding disposition under control, he must devote more persistent attention to it than he had ever given his better self before. Several years later he identified himself closely with all the practical work of the

Second Church, and distinguished himself as being the man of all others who could accept advice without showing impatience.

But the remainder of the club remained faithful, and they devoted themselves to study with an earnestness that was simply magnificent. They would divide each lesson into sections, and assign a section to each member, which member would in turn collect and present to the class all available information upon the subject, and some of the young lady attendants pronounced some of these addresses more interesting than sermons. Mr. Jodderel naturally took in charge all topics relating to the future state of existence, and as the class imposed no arbitrary distinctions as to time, he found no cause to complain. To President Lottson fell the duty of enlightening the class upon the geography of Palestine, and so thoroughly did he do his work that one of his papers was asked for publication, and copies of it were accepted with thanks by several learned societies. Mr.

Prymm, who finally came back to the class after having been assured that for months it had discussed no subject not purely scriptural, made some remarks upon the atonement which were finally collected in a volume entitled " A Layman's Views of Christ's Great Work," and the book received many carefully worded non-committal notices from the religious press, though the bulk of the edition still remains in the storehouse of the publisher. Young Mr. Waggett kept an observant eye for all topics bearing literally upon the subject of salvation. Mr. Hopper found at last an opportunity to read his long-cherished essay upon "The True Location of the Holy Sepulchre," with many notes, suggestions, and emendations by himself. And the class grew in membership and in the number of listeners, and there was never heard in it a personality or a revival of old disputes which had time and again rended the church. Nothing was said in its whole subsequent history which could cast discredit upon the daily life of any member, or cause Satan to feel any serious apprehensions for the continued activity of his own business.

THE END.